THE CRISIS OF INDUSTRIAL SOCIETY

THE CRISIS OF
INDUSTRIAL SOCIETY

Norman Birnbaum

OXFORD UNIVERSITY PRESS

LONDON   OXFORD   NEW YORK

OXFORD UNIVERSITY PRESS

Oxford London New York
Glasgow Toronto Melbourne Wellington
Cape Town Salisbury Ibadan Nairobi Lusaka Addis Ababa
Bombay Calcutta Madras Karachi Lahore Dacca
Kuala Lumpur Hong Kong Tokyo

TO WOLFGANG ABENDROTH AND HERBERT MARCUSE

PREFACE

THIS SET of essays grew out of the lectures I gave at Trinity College during the week in 1967 in which I had the honor to be the annual Lecturer-in-Residence at that distinguished liberal arts college. I exceedingly enjoyed my somewhat strenuous week at Trinity, and learned much in its course. I do wish to thank President (now President Emeritus) Albert Jacobs; Professor Donald Galbraith, Chairman of the Lecture Committee; and Mr. L. Barton Wilson, Director of Public Information, for having done so much to make my visit rewarding. It is a pleasure to thank the students and faculty of Trinity for their personal and intellectual hospitality during my visit. The liberal arts college in its present form is a unique American contribution to higher education. My encounter with Trinity did much to strengthen my conviction that in the present crisis of the universities, institutions like Trinity College are not alone viable, but have much to offer to their larger sisters, by precept and example. I am most appreciative of Trinity College's helpfulness in facilitating the publication of these lectures in their present form.

The ideas contained in these essays were developed, in effect, in collaboration with my colleagues and students at the universities where I taught before moving to Amherst College: Harvard, The London School of Economics and Political Science, Oxford, Strasbourg, Wesleyan, and the Graduate Faculty of the New School for Social Research. I hope that my former colleagues and students will see in these essays at least some of the merits of their own critical observations on earlier formulations of these ideas. I should wish to acknowledge, in particular, the contribution of three of my students at the New School. David Gilbert, Robert Gottlieb, and Gerald Tenny wrote a joint term paper for me which also served as a draft program statement for Students for a Democratic Society, to the benefit of all parties concerned. I owe an especial debt to my former student, research assistant, and colleague in the Five Colleges, Miss Marjorie Childers, of Mount Holyoke College, for her acute and disciplined mustering of materials. I also wish to thank Eric Bohman for his great assistance with the Index.

The observations on universities in the third chapter, particularly, derive from a continuing study of the European and American universities. I am grateful to the Ford Foundation, through its Division of Higher Education and Research, for a grant in aid of these inquiries. My debt to the Foundation will not be discharged until the completion of a book on the universities, but it seems appropriate to record my thanks, initially, here. In this connection the assistance of Marjorie Childers and Edith Kurzweil was considerable.

The essays in this book were, in fact, drafted before the French Revolution of May, 1968, which—despite its disappointing sequel—I consider the most significant event in Western politics in a generation. I did make some minor modifications in the third chapter, especially, in light of these events and did so, in fact, while in Paris in June of 1968. The book as a whole, however, remains substantially unchanged: I must leave it to my readers to judge whether I was any less prescient about the possibility of revolution in the advanced societies than anyone else. I propose to continue my exploration of these themes in a set of essays to be published by Oxford University Press in the Winter of 1970, under the title *Intellectuals, Culture and the New Politics*.

It would be absurd to claim originality for the notions set forth in these pages. I have learned much from many friends and colleagues over the years, especially when their ideas and mine were antithetical. I hope that the bibliography constitutes some formal recognition of my indebtedness to them. I am particularly aware, however, of how much I have gained from my association with Henri Desroche, Lucien Goldmann, Jürgen Habermas, Eric Hobsbawm, Henri Lefebvre, and George Lichtheim. In thanking them here, of course, I absolve them of any responsibilities for the many defects they will no doubt find in the text.

Charles Wright Mills, alas, did not live to see his name mentioned in this connection. Like many in my generation, I owe him a good deal. Finally, I have taken the liberty of dedicating the work to two elder thinkers and friends who have so aided and encouraged many younger than themselves. It is a particular pleasure to do so, since circumstances prevented me from participating in recent *Festschriften* in their honor. Wolfgang Abendroth and Herbert Marcuse once stood at the end of a tradition of critical sociology; by now, they have contributed immensely to its renewal.

N. B.

Amherst, Massachusetts
June 1969

CONTENTS

CONTENTS

THE CRISIS OF INDUSTRIAL SOCIETY

CHAPTER ONE

CLASS

TWO THEMES still mark all discussions of class in industrial society: those of antagonism and collaboration. It is widely believed that an earlier antagonism between the social classes has been replaced by a form of collaboration which, if less dramatic, offers much for all. The increasing productivity of industrial systems, it is argued, enables the working class—previously excluded from anything but a subsistence income—to be quite simply bought into a form of consensus. The complexity and increasing differentiation of occupational structure, moreover, has eliminated the sharp divisions between larger social groupings characteristic of an earlier phase of industrial history: we confront, instead, an intricate network of interconnecting relationships—an almost infinite series of gradations uniting rather than dividing most of industrial society in the enterprise of production, distribution, and administration. One especially ingenuous theory asserts that the considerable residue of class antagonism which remains serves to create a kind of antagonistic collaboration between the social groupings. Precisely by struggling with one another, they create (if unintentionally) permanent modes of co-operation in the solution of common problems.

One of the most remarkable features of the current debate on industrial society is that the same evidence can produce quite opposed conclusions. The very considerable degree of collaboration between social classes which is a visible and pervasive part of the life of our societies can justify an interpretation of the following sort: The mechanisms of integration are so effective, the possibilities of resistance or opposition so reduced—objectively—that men believe what they have to believe, and do what they have to do; it is the era of universal acquiescence, and the social machine functions the more smoothly for it. That the machinery about eliminates the necessity for human choice is, at once, the dreadful and the inevitable price we pay for having the machinery at all. Yet another account might run in this way: The enormous productivity of our system, the value it sets upon individual skills and competence, the way in which it diffuses authority in work and related institutions, allows great increase in concrete freedoms. The integration of each with the system is the precondition, then, of the liberty of all.

The debate on the interpretation of social integration, then, proceeds (except with certain sociologists, who have pronounced themselves for integration and who deny—with an admirable immunity to self-criticism, or indeed to any critical thought whatsoever—that they are engaged in anything but a "scientific" enterprise). The debate's relevance, its pathos, and its obvious interest ought not, however, to blind us to the existence of antagonisms between the classes. Exploitation and domination continue, if in forms not immediately visible except for the cases of those in extreme subordination or in supreme superordination —and except for occasional outbreaks of conflict at intermediate levels in the society. The continuation, also, of profound conflicts of interest (about the rate of increase in productivity as opposed to the somewhat more restrictive interests of *rentiers,* about the division of national income generally and specifically in the form of debates over its allocation for social tasks or consumption) merits our examination. It is in these more profane forms of antagonism, after all, that most of the stuff of modern class conflict can be found. The fact that the conflict is often obscured, that it takes partial and particular forms (not involving whole sectors of society pitted consciously against each other but groupings struggling in limited areas), is evidence for a change in the structure of these conflicts and not, as is vulgarly supposed, evidence for their historical elimination.

One of the great difficulties in treating of social classes in modern society is that the varied nature of the relationships between the classes, combined with their daily proximity, under the influence of the mechanisms which make of society an opaque rather than an open system, render critical analysis difficult. Critical analysis is intrinsically dissensual, and in a world in which facts are their own legitimation, seems increasingly gratuitous or even not a little insane, and is invariably disturbing. Only critical analysis, however, can make sense of the facts, point out their interconnections, relate them to our projects. It remains to examine the commonly accepted notions of the modern class system, to note some difficulties with these, and to use historical perspective to frame a more appropriate view.

One final preliminary difficulty must detain us. The very term "class" is somewhat in dispute. It came into existence first in the nineteenth century, in the turbulence associated with the aftermath of the French Revolution (and the end of the *ancien régime* in Europe) and the rise of new groupings in European society attendant upon the growth of industry. "Class" did not seem to be in use as a descriptive term in the eighteenth century, although John Millar, one of the early Scots sociologists, did use the term "ranks." Marx himself disclaimed having invented the conception "classes," and attributed this to the French liberal historian Guizot. Marx gave a very specific meaning to class: it was a group in common relationship to the means of production and with a developed and active consciousness of that relationship; that is to say, a group which had organized itself to change the relationship (a class "for itself" and not simply "of itself"). With the development of academic sociology devoid of an (obvious) political intention in the decades subsequent to Marx's work, class was emptied of its political meaning. It became any grouping in a similar relationship to the means of production, regardless of the degree of social consciousness or political cohesion it had attained. Occupation, or occupational grouping, has been a common indicator of position with respect to the means of production. Let it be said that this secularized derivative of Marxist theory is the meaning assigned to class in this book, not least because of the apparent failure of the working class to organize itself in such a way that it could fundamentally alter the structure of society.

The phrase "relationship to the means of production" is exceedingly general. The relationships in question can be relationships of ownership, of control, of proximity, of profit. The "means of production" themselves are not unequivocally easy to specify: in addition to machines, these can be extended to the apparatus of distribution and administration, and with the increasing interconnection of state and economy, to political institutions themselves. The indeterminacy of the idea is in one way an advantage: it allows us to take account of the historical transformation of the industrial system itself. (Marx himself referred to "mode of production" or "relationships of production," obviously more general terms for a set of phenomena: the social relationships constructed about the production process itself.)

The present situation, at first glance, is not very difficult to comprehend. In place of old bourgeois elites and old bourgeois groups in the middle of the class structure, new elements have emerged. These new elites are managers of industry, managers in the state sector, entrepreneurial technicians, occasionally politicians. Their characteristic is not the possession of property but its manipulation, not the permanent monopoly of political power but its manipulation as well, their mode of access to reward and privilege not the direct inheritance of a favored position but acquired culture and skill. Beneath them, in an extremely differentiated group extending to or indeed into the skilled working class, is an assemblage of administrators, technicians, service personnel: an army of those skilled in one or another organizational technique, or in more specific techniques placed at the service of organization. Their relationship to the new elites is one of subordination, even if (to some extent) possibilities of ascent into the elites are open. Like the elites above it, the new middle class below it has property mainly in its acquired skills. For both groups, then, education is the privileged mode of access to elite position. For the elites, there are the French *Grandes Ecoles,* the ancient universities in Britain, the Ivy League colleges in the United States— although it should be said (the comparison is frequently made) that the *Grandes Ecoles* give a more specialized and technical education and recruit more explicitly and exclusively on criteria of intellectual merit than do the others. For the new middle class, an entire spectrum of general and specialized institutions provides a minimum of general culture and a maximum of training. Differences of taste, of style, and obvious differences of income separate the groupings; here, too, the phenomena are characterized by gradual transitions and not by excessively sharp disparities.

A similar distinction marks the boundary between the new middle class and the new working class. The rate of expansion of the former is in any case greater than the rate of expansion of the latter. The introduction of new technological processes in industry has changed the character of the more advanced types of industrial work: driving downward into permanent expendability the semi-skilled worker—trained to one job and not capable of mastering new and more global tasks—and raising the level of remuneration and responsibility of the skilled technician. But one factor counteracts the degradation of industrial status suffered by those workers without ability to master new technical processes: the necessity to maintain full or nearly full employment if the economic machinery of capitalism is to turn at all. Relatively free of the cyclical unemployment which was a constant threat to previous generations of workers, and protected (to varying degrees in different countries) by social security systems, the new working class has begun to adopt the habits of consumption of the middle class. Just as the latter is remote in *habitus* from its bourgeois predecessors, the new working class is quite removed from the style of life, the expectations (and the political aggressiveness) of its ancestors. The integrating process which is the chief characteristic of industrial society has now encompassed that class whose inability to integrate into the society was once supposed to destroy that society.

Recent discussion of poverty in the United States (a curious discussion, since the poor existed before they were discovered by politicians, sociologists, and the foundations) does point to an additional phenomenon hard to encompass within the theory of integration: the existence of large numbers of persons who live on the margins of industrial society. The permanently unemployed or the chronically underemployed, those lacking in skills, those in ill health —these have to be distinguished from the new proletariat of imported unskilled workers (the southern Europeans and Africans in western Europe), although they overlap with the reserve army of casual labor available in America's cities. The specially imported labor force aside, it would appear to be true that the new proletariat is outside the society and that its difficulties of integration can be overcome only by special efforts: an increase in the productivity of the industrial machinery would benefit other groupings and not this one, since it has little capacity to seize the opportunities offered by that productivity. That the existence of this group is not necessary to the system may, for the U. S. at least, be suggested by the attractive colored brochure issued by Messrs. Merrill, Lynch, Pierce, Fenner, and Smith: "The New American Horizon." The brochure shows that if there are indeed forty million poor in America, it is clearly in the interests of private enterprise to convert them into forty million customers as soon as possible.

At any rate, the conventional notions are clear. New elite, now middle class, new working class, are of course distinguished by large differences in power, income, and prestige. These distinctions correspond, also, to educational differences: to a considerable extent, education is the mode of access to higher position. The existence of educational opportunity entails an enlargement and a democratization of opportunity (the former British Labour Minister of Education indeed once defined socialism fairly much in this way). The fact is, or is alleged to be, that all three groups now tend a bureaucratic machine. This in itself is a leveling factor: property is increasingly detached from the control of particular persons or groups, and through a variety of mechanisms (nationalization or state supervision) has in effect become increasingly socialized. The new class system allows antagonisms, then, amongst and between groupings in a basically identical position with respect to the means of production. These concern the distribution of the national product, and such aspects of control of the productive process (in a generalized sense) as bears on problems of distribution. The basic issue of stratification, however, has been settled by the technical rationality of the system itself: the division of labor within it is a necessary concomitant of its functioning at all, and none other is conceivable. All classes seem to accept this. The flatness of the historical horizon is perhaps compensated for by the many possibilities for enlarging the human experience within these historical limits. No other society has developed such an immanent and widely accepted philosophy of history: progress, the awareness of it, and an acceptance of the present order of things are here happily combined.

With whatever nuances may be present, this account of the structure of industrial society is accepted by some of its most distinguished contemporary analysts: Bell, Lipset, Riesman, Bazelon, and Galbraith in America; Aron and Crozier in France; Crosland in the United Kingdom; Dahrendorf and Schelsky in Germany. Many of them do, it should be said, seriously criticize the structure of distribution within the society; some ask for new modes of controlling it, in order to effect changes which would increase (in their view) the general good; all seem to accept the notion that things being what they are, they are unlikely to ever be much different.

An alternative sort of interpretation is, however, possible: we may term this critical, in the sense that it takes the modern class structure as given, clearly enough, but not as immutable. It seeks to interpret what the German thinker Hans Heinz Holz has called the "veiled class society," to concentrate on the conflicts and instabilities in the society, on the contradictions between its pretensions and its achievements, between its surface and its depths. Not surprisingly, this sort of interpretation insists on conflict as the prime characteristic of our societies, not on integration—even if the conflict is at times hidden.

Critical analyses of modern society, further, seek new political possibilities, new dimensions of freedom, in its inner movement. At the least, the critical theorists refuse to portray as fixed those constraints which may be transitory —or to depict the attenuated forms of servitude as agencies of political fulfillment. The critical thinkers include Bottomore, Harrington, Heilbroner, Hobsbawn, Lichtheim, Marcuse and O'Brien in the English speaking world; Abendroth, Goldmann, Gorz, Habermas, Lefebvre, Mallet, Mandel, and Touraine on the continent. Clearly, these essays are conceived in terms somewhat like theirs.

We may begin with the question of the new elite. Two problems occur. To what extent is it really new, an elite formed by skill qualifications rather than by inherited position? And to what extent does its function consist in the administration of property rather than in its ownership? The problems are, clearly, connected. If property ownership is still important,. we would expect property owners to be installed at the top of the class system; their managerial employees, however indispensable to them, would manifest different attitudes than those managing impersonal property—or than those managing the economy in the interests of the state. Consider the differences between the ·higher French civil servants working in the Ministry of Finance or the Planning Commission, and the American executives working for the larger corporations. We should, indeed, expect differences between those managing impersonal property in the interest of corporations and those working for the state, despite the frequently remarked interchangeability of personnel between these sectors.

The statistics seem quite unequivocal. The rising levels of consumption attendant upon the recent increments in the productivity of the system have not been accompanied by any serious diminution in inequalities of ownership —except where (as in the western European countries) the state has intervened to confiscate industrial property or to reserve to itself the development of new industries. Indeed, the demands of modern technology seem to require increasing industrial concentration, and profitability depends to a considerable extent upon scale of operations and market domination through size. Are the resultant concentrations of property in the hands of new *rentiers* or do the owners directly manage it? In the first place, there seems to exist something of a symbiosis between managers and *rentiers;* the rewards for management include privileged access to ownership through stock bonuses, share acquisition plans, and the like. In the second place, the impersonal aspects of property entail concentrations of economic power in the control of rather specific sets of managers: bankers, insurance companies, financial consortia. Some managers, in other words, manage more than others—their attitudes would appear to be quite indistinguishable from those of entrepreneurs, except for historical differences which evoke different types of entrepreneurial procedure. Briefly, the notion of higher and lower employees seems exceedingly dubious: there are qualitative differences in the scope of decision, in the consciousness of power, and in the nature of rewards which make the construction of a continuum between the member of the board of directors of a giant financial institution and one of the subordinate officials working in it rather unconvincing. The depersonalization of property does not make the effective control of property less important as a criterion of class differentiation.

If we speak of control of property rather than directly of ownership, what of the problem of access to the group of controllers? Educational opportunity alone does not give us the answer to the problem, and for several reasons. The ability to profit from educational opportunity depends to some considerable extent upon family background; the ability to gain access to some of the more privileged educational institutions does so no less; and there are in addition to formal educational criteria for recruitment to the managerial elite certain criteria of personal comportment and culture which, if somewhat intangible, are no less effectively transmitted by family rather than by any other institution. (In this sense schools, clubs, peer groups, and other educational institutions complement the family as a source of culture rather than replace it.) Briefly, educational stratification is no less effective than many other kinds of division in the class society. The experience of certain societies with opened or enlarged access to elite institutions (the United Kingdom after the educational reforms of 1944 and France through the competitive examinations for admission to the *Grandes Ecoles*) suggests that the institutional reforms adopted may modify but by no means eliminate familial differentials in access. (I propose to deal later on with the question of the content of educational preparation for elites. This varies from nation to nation, and the cultural differences in question often reflect political ones.)

The conspicuous fact about the new form of elite organization is that it is not conspicuous. The general term "manager" or "executive" conceals vast differences of power and influence. The very impersonalization of capital, the sociopolitical semiliteracy of broad strata of the population, makes an adequate popular view of the situation difficult to develop. The intricate network which unites the property managers to the political managers (and to those who command the media of communication) is all the more effective for being informal: not a conspiracy, not even a club, but simply a happy coincidence— a set of common perspectives shared by men well aware of their "responsibilities." Moreover, the intermediate levels of the middle class do enjoy not only excellent income facilities, but certain types of autonomy and scope for decision—as well as the pleasurable sensation of being close to those with more power, or at least closer than many others. The concentration at the top resembles a perfectly plausible division of labor, and the thesis of common participation in a joint enterprise has for some of the servitors of the managerial elite at least a simulacrum of plausibility. The diffusion of share-ownership, particularly in the United States and to a lesser extent in the United Kingdom and West Germany, has not seriously affected the concentration of property—but it has had important social-psychological effects. Moreover, middle-class bureaucratic career progression entails a series of periodic increments in salary and responsibility, with the attendant changes in status: the sense of being allocated from early in occupational life to one rank from which there is little or no escape need not trouble the middle class as much as the working class. The objective situation of dependence may be quite similar, but as yet it has been obscured by certain cultural and psychological correlates of middle-class position.

Higher (and steadier) income, some contact with the elite, a career structure entailing progression, a certain share in prestige, modest status as a *rentier,* then, distinguish the new middle class from the working class. The working class is still, despite a period of prolonged full employment, subject to cyclical fluctuations on the labor market (more so in the United States than in the European societies where the permitted postwar rate of unemployment has been far lower), and is not likely to have a progressive career on the job. Its possibilities of accumulation toward a *rentier* component in its income are very limited, and its total social security benefits—which for the middle class include private as well as state benefits—are lower.

It is true that the rate of increase of the new middle class, in all industrial societies, has been recently greater than the rate of increase in the working class. This, along with the increasing demands placed upon the middle class for education, has resulted in the recent expansion of education—and the public interest in it manifest in every industrial society. The working class, however, has been growing absolutely, due to the continuing decline of the rural population. However, career progression within the working class is generally appreciably less marked than in the middle class and, most important perhaps, opportunity for the exercise of autonomy and (often enough) a sense of the social importance of the specific task are appreciably less. Briefly, the actual work performed by the working class seems to be intrinsically less gratifying and often either onerous or nerve-racking. We shall return to some of these problems when we deal with the theme "culture" (which in no society can be separated from the problem of the meaning of work). For the moment, we can conclude by saying that whatever sense of solidarity may be developed within the working class, in Western societies, at least, its share of general social prestige is smaller than that accruing to the middle class. Whether the working class shares this implicit judgment or not, however, depends upon its own consciousness of its own worth —and this in turn often enough depends upon its political traditions and their role in a distinctively working-class culture.

To this point, we have been considering relationships between the classes rather abstractly—with little reference to the concrete historical differences between societies. The abstract procedure has its advantages, since it does enable us to visualize certain general trends. But a general trend is in fact an extrapolation from a series of specific historical instances, and the differences may be at least as important as their common traits. Moreover, an examination of the differing courses of historical development in industrial societies may enable us to visualize for our own society possibilities seemingly remote when our own history is taken in isolation.

At the beginning of industrial society, in eighteenth-century England, few (if any) contemporaries thought of voluntary integration as an adequate descriptive model for the apprehension of class relationships. The new industrialists, usually located outside London, used the apparatus of repression developed by the agricultural landowners to stave off or put down disturbances amongst the new workers. The lack of a strong centralized state in modern British history, of an apparatus of bureaucrats, has occasionally been adduced to explain both the growth of political freedom in Britain and the lack of hindrance to the full development of unfettered capitalism. About the latter, it may be suggested that the state did often do what had to be done to encourage the capitalists. About the former contention, it may be said that it is quite insufficient: the decentralized state, with those at the top of the local social hierarchy themselves exercising state power (as magistrates, for instance), proved quite effective. The very rapidity of the rate of growth of the new proletariat, its mixed composition (migrants from the countryside, artisans degraded in status and bereft of function, the first generations of offspring born in these circumstances) seemed to pose a threat to the stability of the prevalent order. The encapsulation of that threat, the eventual integration—by comparison—of the British working class in the national community, is due in some large measure not only to relations between the proletariat and the nascent capitalist class, but to the peculiar ties of this last to the earlier elites which ruled Britain.

British history is remarkable in the continuity of its elite structure—precisely through the changes which have seen the displacement of feudal nobility by landed gentry by aristocratic magnates by new capitalists. Since the English Revolution in the seventeenth century, crises and indeed convulsions have characterized transitions within the elite—but a pronounced capacity to assimilate new groups with new modes of procuring wealth has frequently saved old elites from superannuation. The landed aristocracy of the eighteenth century, itself wealthy on account of a mastery of new techniques of husbandry, had many elements who appreciated quickly enough the potential of coal mines, canals, foundries, and factories. It is quite true that many of the new capitalists were risen from the artisanry, or were previously modest traders suddenly come into great wealth on account of the industrial revolution. There was also a grouping of merchant-adventurers involved in overseas and colonial trade and plunder. Religious differences were not unimportant in this complex of groups: Nonconformists were often prominent amongst the new capitalists themselves, Anglicans amongst the older elite elements. We can say that the new men were, for all their brashness, drive, and (often enough) brutality toward the workers, to some extent encumbered by having to fight on two fronts—and to some extent were educated into a different and preindustrial conception of community (if a highly hierarchic and patriarchal one, a gloss for a certain kind of exploitation but a gloss nonetheless). Curious alignments and realignments occurred: generally united with the new capitalists against the threat from below, the older elite elements also tempered their ravenousness by promulgating and exemplifying a different sort of ideology. This tendency found expression later in what was termed "Tory Socialism." We can say that the relationship between the classes in early industrial Britain (well into the second half of the nineteenth century) was not one simply of direct antagonism between a working class and a propertied class but a more complex pattern of conflict.

The inner evolution of the working class also merits our attention. At first recruited from agricultural laborers and rural or small-town artisans, this social stratum throughout the nineteenth century exhibited continuing inner differentiation. The types of industry in which they were employed, the size of the work unit, the nature of the regional culture (in turn effected by these factors), the stability of employment, and the types of work performed within the industry all conditioned different responses to the global society. Trade unionism, it is well known, began amongst the displaced artisans; it was later exceedingly strong amongst the so-called labor aristocrats (well paid, skilled workers). General unionism for less skilled workers came somewhat later. What the nineteenth century did see, in England, was the slow growth of a working-class culture: a distinctive world of response, assumption, and habit formed by the material conditions of working-class existence in a free market society—a society in which market considerations (as well as those of a certain kind of political prudence) had denied the working class formal educational institutions. The working class itself did organize not alone into unions, but into mutual associations for assistance such as the British Friendly Societies, and consumer co-operatives—and this often before rudimentary working-class political organization was developed. These were often based on tightly knit neighborhood and kinship groupings. Demoralization no doubt affected a certain proportion of the world's first working class; but another grouping showed an extraordinary capacity for resistance, even when that resistance took nonpolitical or prepolitical forms.

Meanwhile, the bourgeoisie also changed—with the qualification, of course, that in England it was not a bourgeoisie in the Continental sense, since the self-consciousness and antiaristocratic ideology and culture of the European bourgeoisie was simply missing in the United Kingdom. (The European bourgeoisie was also urban, and the remarkable feature of the development of England was how urbanization was accompanied, for at least the upper reaches of the middle classes, by an attachment to rural models of living.) A strong moral tone, often productive of that moral hypocrisy long associated by England's neighbors with the island people, was the result of the Evangelical movement in the churches. But this religious development was not opposed to aristocratic comportment, since the aristocrats were also often enough Evangelical. There did develop a large middle class that was regionally differentiated: there were north of England local industrialists, and south of England servitors (mainly in the professional classes) of the central elite. There were shopkeepers and merchants, small entrepreneurs, and a growing element of clerks (many of them imported from Germany in the late nineteenth century, on account of deficiencies in England's own educational system). The distinction between a regional and a national class structure was important: the national one was engaged in administration, politics, finance, and, above all, in empire. The local one was engaged in trade, commerce, manufacture. The largest landowners were part of the central elite; many otherwise powerful industrialists were not. The British middle classes as a whole were marked by extreme and intricate nuances of status which at times detracted attention from, but did not entirely obscure, the extreme differences in material condition between the working and middle classes. What they did not obscure was the fact that there was a difference between the middle classes (even those, as the professionals, in close contact with the elite) and the elite itself. This last, with its aristocratic *habitus,* co-opted elements from the middle classes —above all, when they had enough money—but served as a model of culture and behavior for large sectors of a society whose labor force in the late nineteenth century still included some 20 per cent in domestic service. The distinction between local and national elites was particularly important with respect to participation in the governance of empire. While all classes in Britain profited indirectly from this, and while colonial hierarchies mirrored in a curious way those in the homeland, direct control of the empire was in the hands of the magnates. These were an amalgam of old aristocratic and new moneyed (mainly from finance) elements. As we shall see in the chapter on politics, parts at least of the middle classes were not always on the side of the magnates: Gladstone's advocacy of home rule for Ireland, bitterly opposed by the magnates, showed this. But the middle classes—not least through the diffusion of a remarkably pervasive ideology of status and station—usually sided with the magnates against the workers. (But this brings us to questions of politics, and these will come later.)

Class relations in Great Britain during the twentieth century exhibited two contradictory trends. On the one hand, the encapsulation of the working class in its own cultural world continued—mass culture serving to accomplish this in its earlier phases and not to decompose that world, as is sometimes thought. This had its correlate in an intensification of organization into unions, strikes, and political conflict: the Labour Party was formed. On the other hand, social welfare measures and political reform, as well as a gradually rising standard of living, had effects we may term integrating. The use of this term, rather general, can be deceptive: what it does mean is that the working class, through its organizations, settled down to a bitter series of conflicts in which its intention was less the destruction and replacement of British capitalism than its modification. (The early revolutionary ideology of the Labour Party was accompanied, of course, by reformist practice.) There were vast cyclical movements of unemployment, phenomena of direct conflict of a violent kind (particularly in those towns and centers—the Welsh mining districts, the industrial north—in which a largely working-class population dependent upon dominant industries faced a small group of owners and managers, the shock of conflict not having been mediated by the interposition of a larger intermediate grouping or by intermediate structures). The industrial system was, however, changing: Britain was by no means as advanced at this point in terms of technology as Germany (or rather the rate of technological innovation was not as rapid), and the structure of the labor force was less differentiated with respect to skills. Moreover, industrial production was increasingly concentrated but still dispersed in innumerable small industries. "Bloody-mindedness," a peculiarly indigenous term associated with British working-class behavior toward other classes and the larger society, is no doubt a residue (still active) of situations in which the defense of the psychological and economic interests of the class demanded a maximum of hostility and, if necessary, destructiveness. (The diffuse hostility of the working classes to property as such, other persons' property, seems missing in France and Germany—in the latter, just possibly, on account of intact artisanal traditions, in the former possibly because of the relatively recent rural origins of the working class.)

That the British middle class (and, of course, the elite) was convinced that the working class was its enemy is beyond doubt—but this was not infrequently done by defining the national community as one in which the working class ought to know its (subordinate) place. Transgressions were treated as, somehow, unpatriotic: the very sharp repression and (nearly) spontaneous organization of the middle class which met the General Strike of 1926 was justified as an exercise in patriotic and constitutional sentiment, not as the self-conscious expression of class interests.

The persistence of large patches of unemployment in the British economy from the 1920s into the war period meant that large groups of working-class families (sometimes entire communities) lived in conditions of extreme deprivation—a deprivation accentuated by the uneven regional incidence of unemployment, by its concentration in a number of industries, by the obvious security and relative prosperity of the middle classes. For these had, as elsewhere, been growing in number in Britain—despite the deficiencies of a system of education not quite fully public and almost explicitly stratified to meet the requirements (as viewed from above, of course) of the different social groupings. There were, of course, differences in the middle class: the professional groupings had their own middle-class consciousness, as well as very substantial revenues. The lower middle-class may be divided into those subordinated to (and often enough psychologically servile to) the groupings above them (clerks, for example), and those encapsulated between the working class and the middle class proper (such as shopkeepers). The single most conspicuous event in British class relations in the early twentieth century was, of course, the General Strike of 1926: a display of working-class solidarity and of political irresolution by its leaders.

The postwar changes in British society may be seen as entailing an extension of the minimal economic supports already contained in the National Insurance Program to the working class, as generalizing certain social services (chiefly health services) for the whole population, and as marking the beginning of an attempt to broaden the basis of academic recruitment into elite and technological positions. Certain tendencies toward income redistribution were discernible in the period from 1945 to 1952, but these were reversed. The Welfare State profited the middle class at least as much as the working class, and in certain sectors (notably education) even more so: the real beneficiaries of the 1944 Education Act were middle-class families. Two theories of class relations collided in British politics in the 1950s and 1960s—one theory which held that it was the duty of the state to reduce gross discriminations against underprivileged groups, and one theory which held that the state had only to set the framework in which market processes of enrichment would inevitably benefit the underprivileged as well, of course, as everybody else. Affluence amongst the working classes was frequently the result of overtime working, multiple familial employment, and the utilization of new credit arrangements (the installment plan, or hire-purchase in its British name, having come to Britain). A considerable discussion has ensued as to whether this had altered traditional working-class culture, and in particular as to whether such incentives to expenditure as are communicated by the mass media have brought the working class into a middle-class style of life. The discussion does have the merit of showing how superficial some conceptions of "style of life" have been: the acquisition of a certain number of consumer durable goods does not especially alter the market position of the workers, nor give them access to that sort of general culture and education which is increasingly necessary for passage into middle-class types of employment, nor does it constitute the acquisition of property in the sense that property (even life insurance or small-scale shareholdings) can bring income. Being middle class entails the exercise of certain opportunities to accumulate and command; being working class, generally, does not. The peculiar atmosphere and character of relationships between the working class and other classes in Britain reflect the working class's awareness of this: its "bloody-mindedness," a combination of pugnacity, defensiveness, resentment and a keen sense of how to exploit such market advantages as it has;

its insistence on rights and privileges apparently minor ("tea break"); its enjoyment at not "playing the game"— a British middle-class euphemism for the tacit acceptance by anyone of disadvantages as a price of admission to middle-class society.

Structurally, the recent past in England has been accompanied by the usual rise in the tertiary sector, the relative decline of certain extractive and even heavy industries (coal mining and shipbuilding), and a certain migration of industrial labor toward newer industries (electronics and petrochemicals). The traditional sector of the lower middle class has been affected by concentration in retail trading. There has been a growth in technological employment, on the frontiers of what used to be the old working class and the old middle class: these groups seem to comport themselves very much like the new middle class anatomized elsewhere in sociological theory. Their pecuniary rewards are relatively high, their contact with the technical elite is frequent and often close, their general educational preparation rather large, and their culture more like that of the middle class. In England, this has posed certain difficulties: the professions as such were traditionally part of the middle class, but also have been traditionally jealous of their privileges. The acceptance of the technologists as members of the middle class by the old middle class has been slower than the factual progression of the former group in the social structure. It will be seen briefly that a class system is an historical entity: enrooted conceptions, of course serving immediate interests, can make of the same objective situation (the rise of the new middle class) something different in different contexts. Meanwhile, in the elite, the onetime imperial elite has gradually been not quite displaced but somewhat dislodged by a new one with domestic industrial rather than imperial financial-political interests: the returns from domestic commercial television are as important to this new elite as the exploitation of colonial plantations—more so, indeed, in a world in which the former rather than the latter is now a more certain source of profit. It would seem, in short, that England has two class systems which co-exist: one a remnant of imperial England, the other more proper to an insular industrial nation with a highly advanced technology and one which cannot always count upon cheap sources of raw materials from abroad. Class conflict in England, then, is not simply a matter of the opposition of two or three social strata, but is effected by historical memories and forms of ideological response, and frequently is attenuated by the alliances of otherwise opposed classes (industrialists and workers in favor of low interest rates and therefore economic expansion, for instance) dependent upon different economic sectors. The segmentalization of class conflict has progressed through the period since 1945, and on this view, 1926 was not only the climax of a period of extreme class conflict but the beginning of the end of it in its total industrial form. Thereafter, sharp clashes and divisions continued: the specific struggle was restricted to the factory and the general one to Parliament, and the two did not fuse.

Before passing on to France, we need to remind ourselves that in most of European history, great social changes were effected by the state (the rise of the state itself on the ruins of feudalism proper, the French Revolution, the bourgeois state). The supersession of political conflict as a motor of social change or as a mode of social change by conflicts directly involving the market is a brief episode, and only a partial one at that: the state was used (in France until Louis Napoleon in 1864) to repress unionism. The expectation that social change of a violent kind

would split the integument of the state is perhaps a caricature of a liberalism which has been historically superseded itself: monopolies or oligopolies of power remain
in most industrial and capitalist societies as well as in the
other types. Our view that the revolution has somehow
been averted by higher productivity is also not entirely
borne out. Working-class militancy, indeed, has frequently
increased in periods of economic expansion. When we consider a great epoch of expanding unionism, the figures for
every one hundred employees in unions were still small
(1913: France 9, England 25, Germany 28). The conscious
sector of the working class shifted: from the direct descendants of artisans to those in industries with a high concentration of workers, from a libertarian to a bureaucratized
working-class movement, to a direct effort to participate in
the state. This participation in turn modified the class
structure slightly, or at least provided new modalities by
which class conflict could take place. The participation of
working-class political movements in the state has seg-
mented the struggle of the working class (but this was
rarely uniform to begin with) between workplace and the
state itself.

In no country are social and political history so inextricably bound to one another as in France: the French Revolution was long deplored by the right, long utilized as both
a source of inspiration and as a model for new ventures
by the left. The revolution was in fact a social one, and did
displace the landed and court aristocracy in favor of a new
bourgeoisie (although there was a period of restoration in
which old bourgeoisie to some extent became new aristocrats). The stirrings, rumors, conspiracies, and aspirations of "le menu peuple," of all of those who stood with
and to the left of the Jacobins, meanwhile, were a continual source of inspiration to the revolutionary elements

within the working class and the Parisian proletariat: the next revolution would, it was hoped, not leave undone the work of the first. Meanwhile, the revolutionary tradition in the bourgeoisie tempered to some extent the virulence of its opposition to the working class—both claimed legitimacy from the same tradition. Finally, the *étatiste* tradition in the economy meant that the state as source of capital, as regulator of the market, as directing and supervisory agency, was directly implicated in the economy.

The industrial revolution in France was superimposed on the political one: in 1789 there were only about twelve steam engines in France. Indeed, the rate of the industrialization of France was slower than that in England and Germany both: France first became a predominantly urban country in 1954. The peculiarities of French demography may have played some part in this: between 1800 and 1850 the European population expanded by 50 per cent but the French population only by one-third.

The French bourgeoisie, particularly in the nineteenth and early twentieth centuries, was shaped by the matter and memory of its conflict with the aristocracy. One of the causes precipitating the Revolution was an aristocratic attempt to block the ascent of the bourgeoisie into offices previously reserved for the aristocrats. (The pinched condition of the aristocrats also drove them to new rural exactions and so inflamed the peasantry too.) It should not be thought that the aristocracy (only about 1.5 per cent of the population in 1789) monopolized both state offices and land: the bourgeoisie had managed to buy their way into both. Indeed, the bourgeoisie on the eve of the revolution may have owned more land than the aristocracy itself, in the proportions of about 25 per cent to about 20 per cent. The bourgeoisie, of course, was in itself divided: the *haute bourgeoisie* was composed of merchants, professionals, and those in the state service and finances. The *petite bourgeoisie* was so distinct from the haute bourgeoisie that it had its own corporate structure. A sector of the bourgeoisie profited of course from the sale of the *Biens Nationaux* after the revolution; these could not be restored to the aristocracy for fear of offending the bourgeoisie, and the restoration gave the nobles back their titles but not their feudal rights or their property. By 1830, in a France still predominantly agrarian, money was seen politically (no force appeared to save the Bourbons) to be more effective than land. Yet the bourgeoisie continued to put money gained in commerce, manufacturing, finance, and the state service into land. It is interesting that the French term "La Haute Banque" can be used today, as it was used in the nineteenth century, to describe the financial elite of mid-nineteenth-century French society (there was also *la vieille banque* and the new one, frequently developed by Saint-Simonists). The manufacturing and financial elite was small, united by familial ties, and provoked hostility not alone amongst the workers but amongst the lesser bourgeoisie.

The French working class developed rather slowly in the nineteenth century, as a consequence of the relative absence of industrial concentration in the French economy as well as of its still agrarian character. The small enterprise—aside from certain large textile centers such as St. Etienne and those in the east—was most important. As of 1848, workers in large industry represented only a quarter of all workers, the others being dispersed. By 1906 half of the half-industrial labor force was still employed in enterprises employing no more than five persons. The economic condition of the working class was miserable for the first two-thirds of the century, from about 1850 onward; however there were improvements in the worker's condition, despite the maintenance (or indeed widening) of the gap between the incomes of the different classes. The initial leaders of French working-class organization were artisans, carpenters, printers, tailors, hatmakers; and of course the free intellectual atmosphere of Paris made possible the concentration there of revolutionary ideas. Trade-union organization was prohibited until 1864: it was not the "liberal" bourgeoisie, which was liberal with respect to its organization of the economy but less so with respect to threats to its privileges, but Napoleon III who ended the prohibition on unionism. The legalization of unionism did not, of course, reduce the incidence of class conflict. The Paris Commune of 1871 canalized this into political forms, and the working-class movement thereafter carried with it the recollection of the repression inflicted upon the Communards by the bourgeois armed forces.

The Commune having been erased, the working-class movement developed the conception of revolutionary transformation of society by the General Strike—to combine with the daily reality of direct struggles with the *patronat*. The end of the revolutionary tradition begun in 1793 did not mean a total victory for the *grande bourgeoisie:* rather, the consolidation of bourgeois society allowed a whole series of conflicts to be fought out within bourgeois society. Between 1876 and 1913 the number of schoolteachers and civil servants each doubled, and there was an enormous increase in small familial enterprises (to add to the familial peasant enterprises). In short, the epoch was one in which the *petite bourgeoisie* emerged as the great force in French society. Having won universal suffrage and having established the republic, it now concentrated politically on laicism, was drawn to socialism by the positivistic ideals and revolutionary tradition it shared with the socialists, as well as by a distrust of bigness in finance and industry—but was drawn again to the right by its penchant for order and a sense of familistic property. We may say that some of the particular aspects of French industrial society before the First World War were determined by its very large rural component. This relationship has perhaps less to do with attitudes to property (one out of every two French rural families in 1882 was without property), although the tendency to invest in land must have had a certain effect in reducing capital investment in industry, than with attitudes to accumulation and work on the free market. The familistic firm was not particularly dynamic; the aristocratic remnant in the state (in the army and upper bureaucracy, for instance) despised "les affaires"; the *petite bourgeoisie* had an economically conservative psychology; the workers of a highly conscious kind sought the ideal community promised in the not quite extinct visions of the French Revolution's tradition; ties to the countryside and to a still intact rural culture attentuated the exigencies of industrialism; the demographic pulse beat more slowly than in other European societies. The syndicalist ideology of the militant section of the working class, a unionism which did not readily transform itself into an element in a bureaucratic party machine, and the curious idealization of "science" amongst republicans for whom positivism was a duty but to whom industrial technology was not necessarily benign all attest the preindustrial or rather preliberal elements in this Catholic society. The liberalism of the *grande bourgeoisie,* who were not necessarily republicans, did not extend to a generalized politics: this was left for the syndicalists and the *petit bourgeois* democrats. In general, we may say that French society encapsulated industrialism. The *Polytechniciens* amongst the elite and the libertarian syndicalists in the union movement, each in their fashion, conceived of industrialism as a means of extending the national patrimony. The farmers outside industrialization, the *petite bourgeoisie* in their shops and métiers, the *grande bourgeoisie* with their three sets of books (for the government, for the other shareholders, and for the family), the aristocratic remnant in army and state, took a different view.

The period after the First World War, with its terrible price for France, was full of social convulsions. A wave of strikes and a general strike in 1920 were beaten down, and after a period of forward movement in the 1920s the end of the decade witnessed a crippling depression. The election of a Popular Front government in 1936 was followed by a general strike which approached revolutionary dimensions (a compromise was effected by the Popular Front government itself under a socialist prime minister). A counteroffensive led by the *patronat*—who had partly as a result of increasing industrial concentration become better organized—reduced many of these gains. The episode of the Vichy regime saw the *patronat* collaborating with the state, while the bureaucratic elite and the militant sectors of the working class collaborated in the resistance: the campaign of the working class against Vichy was in some significant measure a civil war.

The postwar period, with its planned economic development, social security legislation, migration from the countryside, rationalization of agriculture, severely modified the French class structure. Between 1954 and 1960 the "primary" sector lost 14 per cent of its effectives, the secondary gained 6 per cent, but *"cadres et professions libérales"* gained 31 per cent. As elsewhere, social security seemed to redistribute income within the working class. Meanwhile the independent *petite bourgeoisie* was being replaced by the new middle class which had previously made its appearance elsewhere in large numbers (but which was perhaps more easily absorbed in France because of the importance of the state and state enterprise). The unions showed this interesting pattern: the rate of union membership was above 50 per cent in technologically advanced sectors with high worker qualifications, and about 20 per cent elsewhere. A prominent social historian, Georges Dupeux, has asked whether we may not be witnessing a split between a unionism of "revendication" (hourly and semiskilled workers) and a unionism of "gestion" or autodetermination (more skilled and technically qualified workers). If so, a new sort of labor aristocracy may be at work in an advanced (or neocapitalist) industrial society, this one closely connected with the technical intelligentsia in the new middle class. The demand for a share in the control of enterprises and their long-term policies (including, of course, state enterprises) is obviously a demand which can enlist the support of those who by income and education are members of the bourgeoisie. It is interesting in this connection that the CGT, the French trade union closest to the Communist Party (which has long insisted that only the industrial working class could attain socialism in France) has now begun to publish a rather glossy magazine for "cadres." Here, analysis can only anticipate possible future developments, but it seems that here as elsewhere France may be in advance of other countries.

What may we say in conclusion about the class system in France? In no other country, perhaps, was in the nineteenth century the opposition of aristocracy to bourgeoisie so pronounced; in no other country did the working class feel that the political patrimony of the nation so legitimated its own demands. A very large rural component in the population, meanwhile, and the peculiar form of French industry (its dispersion in many small firms, and the familial character of the large ones) combined to endow French capitalism with a peculiarly static character. Its recent dynamism owes much to an elite of higher civil servants, who have assumed the responsibility for the direction of the whole and who cannot be portrayed as executors of the will of the (transformed) bourgeoisie. The revolutionary impulse of the working class has been so diminished as to be extinguished: new ideas and new movements seem to be concentrated in an advanced group of the working class, and in a technical intelligentsia which on the face of it is part of the bourgeoisie. But the notion of bourgeoisie has been so transformed by events that we may with some justification speak of France as a post-bourgeois society.

These extremely cursory sketches of the development of the modern class system in Britain and France have perhaps at least shown that there is a rather large distinction between the schematic treatment of that system in industrial society and its concrete representation in historical terms. Let us, for the moment, leave aside the vexed questions of the interrelationships between sociology and history as modes of discourse raised by the distinction and content ourselves with some reflections on the future of the class system. I do believe that the historical survey suggests that there are two elements in a situation of class relationship which are sometimes insufficiently taken account of by sociological analysis: political tradition and cultural tradition. Perhaps I can expend some words on each.

By political tradition I mean something other than formal political institutions, or even the balance of political forces in the state. I mean a conception and an experience of state tasks, the peculiar form of embeddedness of the

state in the social structure, and psychological predispositions to use the mechanisms of the state for certain purposes or to have recourse to other institutions (in different traditions) for the same purposes. The political success
of the *petite bourgeoisie* in France clearly owes much to
the relative underdevelopment of industrial capitalism in
that society in the nineteenth century, as compared with
Britain. It also owes something to the ways in which the
revolution, the Napoleonic system, and successive regimes
in the century made of the state not an arbiter between
social classes but an element in the class system itself,
through its economic intervention, its promotion of social
mobility by an educational system far more national than
the British one, its incorporation of a class (the *petite
bourgeoisie* and to some extent the peasant proprietors)
which looked with antagonism on the *Direction des Contributions Directes* but with more positive attitudes to
other aspects of state activity. These popular attitudes,
combined with the conceptions brought to office by the
hautes fonctionnaires, frequently recruited from preindustrial elite families, made of the state and state servitors
elements not imposed on local social groupings, but a force
constitutive of the nation. Even Jowett's men in the administrative class of the British Civil Service never thought
of their work in that way: the British state served the nation, or rather certain conceptions of the national interest
as defined by elites. The allocation to voluntary associations, religious bodies, and local communities of welfare
services and education, and certain traditions of local government (to be sure, frequently rooted in the more
hierarchic aspects of local class systems—in the local domination of landed or industrial families) combined to make
of the British national state in its concrete manifestations
something other than the French state. British conserva-

tism and liberalism in this sense were more nearly like each other than their French counterparts: integralism and Jacobinism.

By cultural tradition I certainly do not mean political ideologies in any narrow sense, but those common systems of meaning by which communities define themselves. Even in a period as secularized as the history of the past century and a half, religious definitions of community have been exceedingly important. Catholicism and Jacobinism in France share this view: they both involve conceptions of national community which depict it as integrated not in the pursuit of sectional or individual ends but in the accomplishment of communal ones. (Jacobinism in its origins was bourgeois, of course, but the French bourgeoisie even at their most anticlerical were spiritual descendants of Catholicism. Liberalism in socio-economic policy in nineteenth-century France, at least, was more nearly an expression of naked class interest than a total ideology— with religious components—in the manner of its British counterpart.) The influence of religious thought on British nineteenth-century social beliefs was both very great and quite explicit: liberalism had a Protestant component; the rigorous acceptance of the dictates of the market was tempered by a certain Evangelical morality. The conception of responsibility had two consequences, one which left the working class to its own devices, and another which demanded that the propertied take some responsibility for the fate of others. The efforts of the British working class to defend itself against the market and its workings were aided to some extent by the beliefs and organizational strength derived from those churches which were part of working-class life, not least the Nonconformist ones. I do not propose to elaborate on these remarks now, but I will assert that the forms and ideologies of class conflict in the two societies can hardly be understood without reference to these elements in the situation.

I wish to conclude this chapter with some observations on the possible future shape of the class system in Western industrial societies. One familiar argument runs as follows: With the change in the composition of the labor force and the enlargement of the new middle class, the character of the elite and of its relationships to its immediate subordinates in the class structure will alter. The old domination of the businessman is in any case eroding: the new managerial elite will be constituted by economists, engineers, and other univeristy-educated specialists. More interested in efficiency and rationality than in a limited sort of profit maximization, bound to their subordinates in the larger private and public bureaucracies by a common education and culture (and frequently enough by the same social origins), the new elite will merge into the new middle class. Meanwhile, the very complexity of the technical operations to be performed at the intermediate levels of the class system, the increasing indispensability of education as a prerequisite for admission to these levels, will inevitably increase the margin of autonomy of those occupying these positions. The argument seems to confuse a number of things. It is quite true that the composition of the elite is changing; it does not follow that the new elite will show greater reluctance to exercise social command than its predecessor. Indeed, its technical competence may increase its sense of legitimacy. Meanwhile, the increasing complexity of economic and administrative tasks may not necessarily accelerate a process of decentralization but may make centralized domination more imperative. The increasing competence of those in intermediate positions in the new class system, then, may be matched by the increasing ability of those above them to command: the relative gap may remain the same. (We have to remember that those in power, in any class system, can usually legitimate themselves by the very fact of their being on top; domination, in one or another form, usually induces consent.)

As for the increase in autonomy, or in the sphere for the exercise of autonomy, of those at middle levels: some have seen in this an objective confirmation of the possibilities of the development of new forms of "participatory democracy." Here, again, the argument is not infrequently confused. Higher education and increasing complexity of occupational task may well evoke a demand on the part of the new middle class for more participation in the economic and administrative command process—but if new rights to participation and new forms of it are to be developed, older systems of command will have to be attacked frontally. They can be replaced, in theory, with devices like participation by the work force in the planning of the program of the enterprise, by mechanisms for the election of those in command positions and the development of bodies which could control their decisions, by the generalization of these innovations to the entire administrative-economic structure through a (democratically conceived) planning body. Innovations of this sort would presuppose a political will to change in the new middle class (and in at least some sectors of the elite) which is, for the moment at least, quite indiscernible. The political consciousness of the new middle class, when it takes a direction which can in a very minimal sense be deemed radical, has been canalized into the usual forms of political action and has been concerned with the usual uses of the state to modify certain conditions uncongenial to the group: in this sense Kennedyism may be thought of as a doctrine of an America fit for the educated middle class to live in.

The situation in France, needless to add, is somewhat more advanced: there, the most advanced groupings in the intelligentsia are quite actively seeking a model for new forms of democracy (frequently, these groups are found amongst left Catholics, and the Mendesiste faction of the technocrats—hardly amongst Communists). At any rate, in America, the new middle class has as yet to indicate—the activities of its children in the universities, to the contrary, notwithstanding—the least receptivity to these notions. Indeed, it has only begun to develop an interest in white-collar trade unionism, a trade unionism which like its working class counterpart hardly ever demands fundamental changes in relationships of domination in the workplace.

Of the manual working class itself, only the following need now be said. Its relative constriction in numbers will not, of course, make it less militant, and there is some evidence that it will render it more so. But militancy, here, will frequently have the character of a rear-guard action, the defense of acquired positions, or a craft-like attempt to control access to a limited set of privileges. The change in technical composition of the upper reaches of the working class (from skilled workers to technicians whose training, remuneration, and task autonomy might be thought to place them in the lower reaches of the technical intelligentsia) may not have radical political consequences: it might result in a more pervasive form of *embourgeoisement* in which middle-class career patterns and attitudes to economic authority replace working-class militancy. (The cases of France, with its *syndicalisme de gestion,* and of technicians' unions like ASSET in Britain suggest the opposite—but these are societies in which a socialist tradition exists to be modernized.) However, there is some evidence (from Europe, chiefly) that affluence and *embour-*

geoisement do not render certain groups of workers any less militant in their political-economic attitudes, that the political recognition of a condition of subordination in the total society remains with a working class with a socialist tradition.

One conclusion suggests itself, and perhaps a surprising one for those who take too vulgar a view of the effects of class systems on consciousness. Not unrefined experience alone but conscious reflection upon it, not the immanence of an historical situation but the cultural perspectives with which a new generation interprets it, may be decisive for the emergence of new forms of social consciousness. Viewed in this way, the United States, for all of its technological modernity, remains by contrast with western Europe a culturally backward society. The cultural means to master the new forms of domination developed in late industrial society may or may not be available in those (considerable) remnants of European bourgeois culture which are still vital; they seem conspicuously absent in the United States.

CHAPTER TWO

POWER

ABOUT THE broad outlines, if not the inner tendencies of development, of the industrial class system there can be little doubt. About politics in industrial society, debate continues unchecked, particularly where the exercise of power is veiled, even denied by those who exert it; where the ephemera of politics and the surface play of the political elements concentrate attention upon themselves; where political decisions are influenced, nay determined, by events and alignments of forces in spheres ostensibly remote from the workings of the state; where, on the contrary, the state is so inextricably linked to other institutions that its distinctiveness is no longer obvious—there are many reasons for the continuation of debate. Moreover, those party to the debate are themselves politically engaged, in favor of one or another version of the good society—or resigned, at least, to living with present ills rather than seeking future cures. In nearly every case of analysis, a moral judgment as to the use of power is made, a moral judgment often enough fused with a set of political preferences of an extremely concrete kind. The statement of a political possibility is not alone a consequence of the analysis of the factual elements in a situation, but a product of a political vision—even where the vision is of an extremely flat kind and consists only of the conviction that things are likely to remain as they are or become more so. These two elements, then—the actual obscurity of the object, and the limited perspectives of those examining it —contribute to the difficulty of analyzing power in industrial society.

The new industrial state, it should be recalled, emerged at a time when the absolutistic state was in any case being rent asunder. The absolutistic state had created, and in part was created by, a stratum which was composed of landed and commercial elements: they served the crown to protect and enlarge their interests. These were not always identical with those of the state bureaucracy and the court, although often they tended to merge, and with the desacralization of politics in the seventeenth and eighteenth centuries the reflective (and reflecting) elite of Europe developed an uncomfortable awareness of the distinction between state and society. If a Montesquieu depicted political institutions, social order, and historical circumstances as in a rough correspondence, his contemporaries were beginning to insist on the distinction between state and society. One of the most influential treatises of the eighteenth century was Ferguson's "An Essay on the History of Civil Society," the very title of which indicated the author's intention: to depict a continuity in social life independent of variations in state forms. Those chiefly responsible for this new awareness of a conflict between state and society were often enough opponents of the absolutistic state, or those who envisaged the development of the common good by alternative means: by the market or by common economic institutions. But there were also thinkers who insisted on the primacy of institutions and elements like the family, or culture, or a national character—precisely to allow some room for organic development and spontaneity in society. Thought at the end of the eighteenth century reflected a process already at the center of European history: the struggle to occupy and alter the structures of power.

If a state were to be changed, and if society were independent of the state, then clearly the direction of the change depended upon the balance of forces in the society. This was not an abstract or purely theoretical question: while political philosophers and social thinkers generally argued about these matters—not infrequently, they argued past each other (Herder and Rousseau, Marx and Mill, Nietzsche and Spencer, Veblen and Sorel were contemporaries)—history was changing the terms of the discussion. The eighteenth century was the last century of pure political discourse, and even then it was mitigated, amended, and modified by admixtures of sociological and historical reasoning. The decomposition of the old relationships, the uncertainty of the new ones, and the decisive impulse to a new kind of political reasoning (from society to state rather than from state to society) was given by the French Revolution. The French Revolution preceded, in France and on the continent, the industrial one—but it so shook the *ancien régime* (and not only in France) that for two generations thereafter those who had charged themselves with the defense of established interests were careful to look for other interests with which they might ally themselves for mutual survival. De Tocqueville amongst others held that the revolution and the Napoleonic state fulfilled the tasks of the *ancien régime* in France, that it centralized administration, destroyed local aristocratic powers, and raised the state above the nation so that contending national factions could contend for the state. He was right, perhaps, to insist on continuity in European political history—but the element of discontinuity was to be found in the explicitness with which political power was now derived from other forms of social domination. Insofar as that domination was resisted, the state was in danger: The French Revolution, by generalizing resistance, generalized political disturbance.

The steam engine, the spinning jenny, the iron foundry, and the railroad constituted the armature of a new society. New propertied elements, if in alliance with the old, and new exploited strata, if kin to the underprivileged in pre-industrial Europe (with whom for a time they existed side by side) assumed new political roles. It would be wrong to suppose that they immediately displaced their predecessors; rather, they became entangled with them in a new system of politics. Just as class conflict in nineteenth-century Europe saw the new industrial classes in conflict not only with each other but with the preindustrial ones, the struggle for the state reproduced these same alignments. One paradoxical result of the process has been this: society in the industrial epoch has at times seemed to replace state functions by its own, or to fulfill tasks beyond the capacity or competence of the state. If this describes the beginning of industrial society, it can no longer be said to be true. As industrial society has developed, functions once fulfilled by the market and by unplanned social arrangements have increasingly devolved upon the state. Until very recently, indeed, it appeared that the state's exercise of power was intensifying in all spheres: the necessity of warding off threats to property turned the propertied to the state, and in the various forms of repressive capitalism (as in fascism) the organized working class was opposed with brute force. Periodicities in the openness and violence of conflict have been frequent: we are today in an epoch of integration, of more or less peaceful acceptance of the class structure by a working class psychologically assimilated into the political system. It does not follow that assimilation is complete or irreversible. It is remarkable, however, that as co-ordination and direction devolve upon the state, internal coercion seems less imperative: it has been replaced by psychological compliance, whose roots are varied. A generation ago, French and American workers were occupying factories, and the German working-class movement had been destroyed by a savage counterrevolution, a sullen British working class was recovering from the political arrangements made by those who had once led it, and the Stalinist purges in the Soviet Union were near the culminating point of their murderous frenzy. The very enumeration of these facts gives matter for thought. Whether and how another set of changes may come upon us is a matter that can be considered later: for the moment, let us examine how we arrived at our present position.

I

The new industrial classes had to contend, for control of the state, with preindustrial ones. Moreover, a group which I shall designate as a state bourgeoisie (a group whose income, prestige, and power depended upon its access to positions in the state's hierarchy) had managed to establish itself as a political elite. The precise relationship of the elite to groups dominant in agriculture, industry, or commerce (as well as in the spheres of culture and ideology) remains a question: whatever influence or control these groups exercised upon the political elite, there can be little doubt that for periods the political elite could act in a relatively self-contained manner. The gradual substitution through change in the basis of recruitment to the political elite from the landed aristocracy to the industrial bourgeoisie, the more or less open purchase of political favors by the bourgeoisie, the development of new forms of political recourse (parliamentary institutions or the development of a public opinion influenced by the press, as well as by contacts in face to face and community groupings) altered the character of the state. It may be said, parenthetically, that with the exception of certain smaller countries, the share of the working class in the governance of the industrial nations has remained disproportionately small: the working class as such has not managed to embed itself in state institutions, the proportions of persons of working-class origins who occupy posts in the state bureaucracies are small (and when such persons are found, their ties to the working class are usually attenuated), and Social Democratic regimes have not very much altered the character of states which are fundamentally integrated with other classes. We shall have to consider to what extent the apparatus of the state may be deemed independent of the class context in which it operates, and to what extent, therefore, political power may modify the opportunities for domination given by market relationships. At the extremes, with one or another class totally controlling the state and acting with unequivocal ruthlessness toward any (social or political) opposition, the state may be thought of as subject to class domination. However, moments of extreme crystallization of this sort are not frequent, and we shall therefore have to examine situations in which domination is modified or opaque.

The most practicable method to follow in dealing with these questions is in fact to survey the transformations in the political elite—and above all, elite structures—attendant upon industrialization. We may begin with Britain. There, in the eighteenth century, a system of judicious local repression, of purchase of office and other forms or corruption, of restricted suffrage and electoral manipu-

lation, allowed the landed aristocracy to dominate government and Parliament. The nascent industrial class did not
break into the state until the nineteenth century. It coa-
lesced with the landed aristocracy to avert the threat of a
revolution, but generated enough pressure to effect electoral reforms and the critical alteration in tariff arrangements—the repeal of the Corn Laws, which meant that
cheap food from abroad was preferred to the protection of
domestic agriculture. One of the striking features of British political development in the nineteenth century was
precisely its lack of evenness: the landed aristocracy and its
political representatives maintained central power, in
government and state office, beyond the point in time at
which the industrialists were in fact locally dominant. The
Civil Service Reforms of mid-century, the late nineteenth-
century changes in the composition of the Tory Party, the
development of urban political machines led by the business class, marked the formal entry of new industrial
groups into the national political elite: at the local level,
through the magistracy and its control of the police, they
had in any case exercised power. As the agitated conflicts
surrounding the Reform Act of 1906 showed (the Liberals
had in effect to threaten to wipe out the House of Lords to
reduce its resistance to reform), the landed aristocracy did
not relinquish control lightly. By this time, however, it
had in fact become an imperial elite: the state, relatively
liberal within, was used to maintain situations favorable to
the acquisition of booty and the extension of markets
abroad. Whether the concentration of repression abroad,
or on ethnically distinct groups (in Britain in the Empire
and on the Irish, in America on the Indians and Negroes,
in France on the Maghreb and later West Africa and Indo-
china) allowed a certain liberalism with respect to the
national community (either by cementing it in some way,

or by focusing aggression outward—another way, perhaps, of saying the same thing) is a question which ought to be posed. At any rate, for Britain the state did not pass directly from the landed aristocracy to the new industrial bourgeoisie; it underwent two sorts of transformations. In the first instance, the urban middle classes, professionals and gentry, provided—aided by the ideology of service derived from Evangelical versions of Protestantism—a new set of state servitors, who were certainly not burdened with critical ideas or inclinations to radicalize the social order, but who were not crude servitors of industrial wealth, either. Secondly, the older landed aristocracy became an imperial elite: magnates whose economic activities had shifted to city finance and whose political ones extended overseas to the control of empire. These two elements, a set of middle-class bureaucrats and publicists and the imperial magnates, were both interested (if for somewhat different reasons) in social cohesion at home. They directed the state's affairs in collaboration with the industrialists, but at something of a distance from them. A political elite, then, can serve the interests of a propertied bourgeoisie even when maintaining its distinctiveness from it.

The British case is particularly instructive because of its liberal ideological and institutional components. The formal role of government was no doubt somewhat less than it was in societies like France and Germany: in particular, government's economic role was less. Spencer, indeed, opposed Britain to France and Germany, the one as an "industrial" or liberal society working by contract, the others as "military" or authoritarian and centralized, directed societies working by regimentation. (The France he was describing was largely the France of Napoleon III!) But the institution of contract, as the role of the courts in labor disputes showed, could involve recourse to the state power to legitimate and reinforce situations of domination through the market. The organization of power enabled local elites to penetrate the machinery of government and justice. The inimitable British mechanisms of consensus through a system of elite cultural communications (group ties joined in a small number of schools and in the ancient universities, in London society, in Parliament) united these local oligarchs across the nation. The state as such was not very visible in the provinces, but the absence of violent contention for its control amongst elite groups perhaps accounted for both its pervasive and its opaque qualities. Briefly, British society left to itself seemed to generate mechanisms of control which made an enlargement of state tasks gratuitous: in this sense, Spencer was quite right to view the market as decisive. It is, however, important to see that in the country with the most developed market, the domination of the state by market mechanisms was most complete, or rather the substitution for central political control of economic compulsion and the local enforcement of that compulsion. It would be false, however, to assert a connection between the minimization of state power and the completion of the process of industrialization. Other societies took different courses of development.

In Germany, the industrial revolution was accomplished in direct conjunction with the state. The Prussian state in particular was the property of a landed and bureaucratic aristocracy which colonized it: the higher educational system produced officials, the popular educational system (the first public system in Europe) produced soldiers and artisans. The new industrial bourgeoisie and the mercantile and commerical classes had to accept the political leadership of a stratum with different historical experiences.

What was remarkable was the way in which the state aristocracy made the transition from commanding an agricultural society to directing an industrial one. The avoidance of the conflicts within old and new elites which so disturbed British and French political life seemed due to the national factor: social and national development depended upon national unification, and the Prussian elite which provided it assumed other command positions as well. The structure of German industry mirrored the structure of German administration: if the family firm characterized French industry, German industry was marked very early by cartelization—by economic combines which worked with the state. The alliance of agricultural capitalists, state officials (including army officers and university professors), and industrialists provided the elements of the modern German elite: it is clear that the *petite bourgeoisie* in the state and small enterprise was increasingly incorporated in this system (the latter on account of their dependence on bank credit, banking having been centralized early in Germany). They could not, as in France, develop an independent political ethic. The eventual struggle for democracy in Germany devolved very largely upon the working class, for whom parliamentary representation and the strengthening of Parliament vis-à-vis the crown and government were conditions of incorporation into the political community at all. It should be remembered that the peasantry in Germany could be relied upon—a point Max Weber saw clearly—for service to the elite. The state institutions of Germany were sufficiently strong to withstand the divisiveness of the *Kulturkampf* which opposed state and Protestant Germany to Catholicism, and were devised to exclude the working-class movement except for the institution in which control of the state was weakest: Parliament. The industrial bourgeoisie was not liberal because it was protected by a state based on nonindustrial elements. There was no alliance of the "industrial" classes against nonindustrial ones because the state was so completely in the hands of the latter, who chose to extend protection to the industrialists precisely if they refrained from liberal politics. The space in which British liberalism grew was simply too constricted in Germany—and the religious configuration excluded it, as well.

In France, the industrial classes were (as we have seen) slow to develop. The state from the fall of Napoleon onward was the locus of a struggle between elements in the bourgeoisie: the older, locally based landed ones, the newer Parisian bankers, the urban *petite bourgeoisie,* and the peasant proprietors. The sequence of revolutions and counterrevolutions in 1830, 1848-51, 1871, witnessed an increasingly important participation of the working class; but in the end this class was powerless to assume command of the state itself, and alternately frightened the *petite bourgeoisie* and peasantry into siding with the more powerful elements in society or lent the former support which tempered the rule of the latter. It was not until the Third Republic that the *petite bourgeoisie* and peasants allied themselves in radicalism to seize command of the state, and this was not unchallenged by older elements (the upper bourgeoisie, the army) who mounted a continuous campaign against them. The typical state servitor in nineteenth-century France was, until the policy of public educational recruitment for these posts toward its end, from the older parts of the *bourgeoisie* (the army remained a particular fortress of these elements). The Dreyfus case seemed to bring to the surface all the contending elements in a crisis of political self-definition: republicans and antirepublicans, clericalists and anticlericalists, older and upper bourgeoisie and *petite bourgeoisie* (many of whom in the provinces were of course anti-Dreyfusard). What happened in France was that parliamentary democracy triumphed without liberalism; the radicalism of the victorious element was a compound of ideological rationalism, *étatisme,* and conservatism with respect to the control and possession of property. A nation of *petite bourgeoisie* and petty proprietors, of civil servants, encapsulated the socialist threat from the working class and the threat of reaction from the nostalgic servitors of older ideals. The industrial bourgeoisie no doubt would, if pressed, have elected "order." Order in France was ultimately guaranteed by parliamentary democracy and not (as in Germany) by an autocracy to which the industrialists could attach themselves. It must also be remembered that in France the industrial bourgeoisie was weak, weaker than in England, Germany, or America. An alliance of the industrial bourgeoisie with other elements against the republic would have mobilized small-scale property owners against itself. The latter had fears focused on the memories of the Commune and anticipations of a general working-class rising, which precluded a total alliance with the working class— but it entered a political and eventually a parliamentary alliance with the workers.

The struggle for control of the state in the United States entailed different forces. The merchants of New England and the planters of the south were not quite the equivalents of the European state *bourgeoisie*—even if they did make the early American state their own. With the triumph of Jacksonian democracy in the early nineteenth century, the agrarians assumed command: it should not be thought that these were simple farmers, for they were all who wished a rapid expansion into the west, and this included the nascent industrial stratum. It is quite true that there were short-term conflicts over any number of issues: the long-run interests of the western agrarians and of the industrialists did not conflict in the period of westward expansion and market development.

Early politics in America were dominated by northern merchants and southern planters. The Jacksonian triumph seemed to mean that the New World would not repeat the fatality of the old, that a genuine popular democracy had been born: De Tocqueville's work on America reflected this impression. In fact, the Jacksonian triumph was an episode: the opening of the west and the momentary triumph of western agrarian populations meant that unprecedented opportunities were open for economic development. These in turn brought to the surface a set of politicians subservient to business and enterprise. The rise of American industry was accompanied by corruption on a gigantic scale, by the replacement of the patrician elite by men of coarser manners and less restrained morals, by the decline of early American notions of the commonweal and the development of a political ideology which was so extreme in its demand that the market dominate the state that it constituted a caricature of liberalism.

The Civil War and the destruction of southern agrarian political power—or, in view of the restoration of southern white domination, of slave power and its replacement by agricultural capitalist power—was not entirely the work of northern business. Western farmers fearful of the intrusion of slave labor into their states and territories, the educated northern middle class with its ethical aversion to slavery, provided the moral support for the war. Business, if anything, attempted to avoid it. But once begun, the war facilitated the development of business. The classical period of American capitalist expansion, between the Civil War and the turn of the twentieth century, was one in which the new entrepreneurial elite (in the absence of a countervailing power from other sections of the middle classes, and in view of the weakness of the working class and the division of the agrarian population) simply worked with and through the state. Lands were, for instance, given to the railroads on a very large scale; the most rudimentary legislation to protect the working class was blocked; regulation of those whose market manipulations (the price of railroad grain loadings, for instance) affected the farmers was derisory or nonexistent.

The educated patricians watched with revulsion as *homines novi* occupied the state. The latter were supported by the southern agrarian elite; had not northern business in effect refused to confiscate their property during the debates over reconstruction, for fear of the general effects of this move on property? The possible sources of opposition were ineffective. The working class was ethnically divided, a very considerable factor in the history of the American working-class movement: vertical organization became exceedingly difficult. In the cities, the political machines disciplined and enveloped the immigrant masses: corruption was a small price to pay for the business class if in fact the antibusiness potential of the urban areas could be neutralized in this way. The agrarian population was stirred by waves of protest, but as the urban population grew, the agrarian movement was incapable of making common cause with it: nativistic and xenophobic sentiments, as well as conflicts of interest, accounted for this. The whole was bound together, if that is the term, by an individualized ideology which defined proper community action as action within a market framework. The very few intellectuals who, at the beginning of the twentieth century, combined native egalitarianism with sophisticated conceptions of political economy derived from the European (mainly German) universities were without immediate political influence. The American state developed, well into the modern epoch, as an ancillary of the market.

This brief summary of the development of the state in four industrial societies allows a number of conclusions. Power was not in the nineteenth century immediately and totally derived from domination of the market. Preindustrial elites often enough shared power with the industrial bourgeoisie and in the cases of Britain and Germany modified its ascendancy. Political traditions, as in France, provided an ideological prism through which class conflict was refracted—although, of course, political traditions are the legacies of previous class conflicts. In due course, the preindustrial elites of Germany and Britain altered their character and political direction: they became less concerned with the defense of acquired agrarian interests and more with the position of the state vis-à-vis a world market, that is to say, they became imperialist. Only in the United States did the market seem to work directly: here there were preindustrial traditions, but these were weak, and in the form of the southern slaveholding elite, they were militarily destroyed. The state in America was in effect bought by the capitalist elite, and it was used to destroy not only the southern slaveholders but the North Americans who stood in the way of the westward expansion of the economy.

It will be seen that this account of the development of the state in industrial society has ignored the gradual extension of universal suffrage, the increasing incorporation of previously excluded groups in the political system—the possible modification, in other words, of market and elite domination by the mechanisms of democratic political conflict. It is to this theme that I now turn.

The history of industrial society is not the history of the extension of liberty. Gross and violent forms of domination

have emerged in combination with technologically per-
fected means for the exercise of power; more subtle
forms of domination have politicized the totality of culture. Where liberty has been extended, it has in fact been
won in conflict, conflict which frequently entailed violence
or the threat of it. If the market has been tempered in its
workings, this has been due mainly to the power exercised
by the organized working class: the preindustrial ideas of
community found amongst certain elites have been important, but these elites have made common cause with those
with industrial property as often as they have persuaded
the latter to timely concessions. To what extent preindustrial notions of community (including secularized derivatives of religious beliefs) have found their way into socialist imperatives adapted by the working class is a question best dealt with under the rubric of culture: we deal
here with power primarily and its legitimation only sec-
ondarily.

The socialist movement has been the political expression
of a certain interpretation of the conflict between social
classes. Let us say that it has constituted a series of interpretations, sometimes contradictory, often conflicting, and
always cast in national political idioms and subject both to
the vagaries and regularities of national political tradition
and history. The socialist movement has in its total aspirations for the capitalist nations failed: that failure, however,
contains many elements of success. The extension of universal suffrage owes much to socialist pressure; successive
modifications of the unlimited domination of the economy
by purely market considerations do so as well; and the rationality which can within limits be ascribed to some of
contemporary capitalism is in part borrowed from socialist
ideas. The reconstruction of society and a new human
epoch remain to be accomplished: meanwhile, the state

remains allied to property but here and there shows signs of detaching itself, not to serve as an agency of conscious transformation but to mediate between the conflicting interests of property and a public which includes, but is by no means dominated by, the organized working class. With changes in the composition of the labor force, the industrial working class has diminished in importance and in political weight: the problem of the conversion to socialism of the new middle class, of those who are workers in all but name and consciousness, remains unsolved. It will have to be a new sort of socialism, a neosocialism to go with neocapitalism; but we are running ahead of the argument.

The socialist movement had originally two political components. One demanded the destruction of the state itself as oppressive, the transfer of political functions to work groups which could directly control production and distribution and which could also serve as means for the expression and execution of political decision. We may recognize in this a tendency which goes back beyond industrialization to the European guild tradition: the guilds were occupational and political groups. Curiously enough, this tradition also attracted modernists like Saint-Simon, who identified themselves not with the working class but with the new entrepreneurs and industrialists. In the socialist version, the tradition of direct control has had most influence in the Latin countries, in the form of syndicalism. (The Soviets in early revolutionary Russia were superseded by the centralized state.) The other tradition did indeed envisage the destruction of the state, but after a period in which the state itself would serve as a medium of transformation, forcibly altering society in a socialist direction. The socialist successes attained to date seem to rest on the development of this last tradition, on the utilization of the state to modify the rigors of the market. The state utilized by the socialist movement remains the bourgeois state, and the acceptance by this movement of the conventional terms of politics has been accompanied by a severe diminution in the movement's claims to be able to transform society totally. It must be said, however, that integration in the sense of the integration of the working class in politics is not simply a one-way process: the prevailing definitions of politics, the limits of political participation, had to be widened before integration could take place. As we shall see, that integration is by no means complete, and future developments might well modify it and the entire course of industrial politics.

II

The discussion thus far has been historical; indeed, it has been an historical treatise on the state, its change in composition and function from the eighteenth to the early twentieth century. I have, it seems, accepted (for all the attention given to the classical tradition in political philosophy, with its emphasis on the relationship of state to society, and its transmutation into sociology, with its emphasis on the relationship of society to the state) the conventional notion that the state is the locus of power in society. I do indeed accept this notion, and I find misleading a political sociology which deals with the dispersion and fragmentation of power (or, worse yet, attempts to interpret political process in the state with its centralizing functions for the national community as equivalent to power relations in the other institutions of society) to the exclusion of its centralization in the state. The idea of the centralization of power in the state, it must be said, by no means excludes an analysis of the forces which shape or determine the exercise of power in the state; it does give a definite historical and institutional focus to the discussion.

The history of the twentieth century has been a history of immense and rapid social changes, of violent internecine warfare within advanced societies as well as brutal struggles between them, of the emergence of a social machinery of unprecedented complexity and opaqueness, accompanied by the development and release of psycho-social forces whose intensity has been matched historically but whose quantitative extension in modern populations is new. The productive and administrative processes have increasingly tended to merge, the market (thought in the nineteenth century to be the supremely self-regulating social institution) has been unable to execute its (self-assigned) tasks of economic administration. In the circumstances, the co-ordinating and steering function of the industrial state has become dominant. Where a nineteenth-century thinker like Spencer could suppose that industrial societies in their most essential form would devolve their co-ordinating and steering tasks upon several institutions, and that centralized authority and hierarchy would be minimized by contrast with their omnipresence in what he termed military societies, we have in fact witnessed the erosion, if not the extirpation, of liberal anticipations of a decentralized and pluralistic social order.

Before we examine the actual contours of the contemporary industrial state, we ought to clarify the bases of political order in industrial societies. We touch on themes which are often in the province of political philosophy: the nature of the political order (as distinguished from other social orders), the justification for it, the legitimation of obedience (and of dissent). I do not propose to make a philosophical excursus. I do think it wise to deal with some traditional questions of political philosophy, insofar as these affect the modern state, in a socio-historical manner. The questions are exceedingly relevant, since we cannot understand the functioning of the state apparatus unless we have some views about the types of consensus or dissensus which accompany it. I do not ask, under what circumstances ought men to obey, and to what extent ought the state to regulate their lives? I do ask, why do they obey, and to what extent does the state impinge upon them?

A traditional definition of the state has been that it is the institution with a monopoly on the legitimate use of violence. An equally traditional view, or rather an extremely conventional one, is that internal violence has tended to diminish with what is termed progress. Indeed the view was accepted, as late as 1931, by Sigmund Freud, who in *Civilization and Its Discontents* argued that the diminution of visible and behavioral violence demanded and imposed by civilization heightened intrapsychic repression. Historically, it is difficult to accept the assertion that violence has diminished. The test of the proposition is not, perhaps, the existence of routine (which is accounted for by a variety of consensual processes) but those moments when the social order or important constituents of it are challenged. Class conflict which threatens property, linguistic or ethnic conflict which threatens the maintenance of the state itself, the peculiar intensities of the American racial conflict (which combines class and ethnic conflict), and major political opposition when it attains a point at which the conduct of government seems about to be rendered impossible—these are occasions on which states continue to employ violence. Moreover, the maintenance of extensive internal police forces constitutes a continuing institutional preparation for violence; there is clearly no evidence that in terms of efficacy or readiness to intervene, the role of such forces has diminished in industrial societies.

The standard treatment of crime in sociological literature as a form of "social pathology" overlooks some of the political elements in criminal activity. In the first instance, a certain amount of crime is in fact a form of class conflict, a continuing war of the poor against not the rich but those richer than themselves. Secondly, there are instances of criminality aligned with parts of the state apparatus and the political system (the American urban political machine, the Mafia in Sicily—which pursued, let it be said, a particularly vigorous and unequivocal policy of opposition to the Italian Communist Party by systematically murdering local Communist leaders). Thirdly, new instances of highly organized criminal business enterprises, with a reinvestment of profits from spheres like drug traffic and prostitution in somewhat more respectable enterprises (transport and the like), demand a minimum of collaboration of the criminal leadership with state agencies. The frequent devolution of the task of policing the criminal milieu in relatively orderly fashion upon criminals working tacitly or openly with the police suggests that the state can utilize even criminal violence for its ends. In general, we may say that any careful examination of the daily activities of the police in an orderly industrial society will show how much repeated and extreme violence is in fact normal for a society of this sort.

The propensity of industrial society to the utilization of internal violence is of course not exhausted by occasional threats to the social order or the continuing threat and problem of encapsulation of criminal violence. For long periods of history in the nineteenth and twentieth centuries, the state maintained itself by the repeated and open use of political violence. The limitation of rights of political representation to a fraction of the population in the nineteenth and early twentieth centuries was altered not only by the ideological evolution of the political elites involved, but by the threat and actual use of counterviolence by the disenfranchised. The celebrated specter of the general strike was more than a figment of the imagination of febrile agitators or overanxious defenders of property. We shall see that the failure of this strike to materialize at the outbreak of the First World War, when it was expected by socialist leaders to halt the conflict, posed in extreme fashion the question of the consensual ideologies which were far more effective than working class internationalism. Internally, however, the working classes remained threats to the elites in command of the several state systems. Even as relatively tranquil a society as Britain (whose tranquillity, to be sure, has been more often a constituent element in the ideology of the British elite than a prominent aspect of British social life) experienced a general strike in 1926, in which large numbers of persons from the middle classes were mobilized to reinforce the apparatus of repression of the state. The chief modern example of the practice of institutionalized and open violence by the state in relatively advanced societies will, of course, be found in fascism.

I use the generic term "fascism" to encompass a variety of movements and regimes whose historical coloration and structures are distinct. Mussolini's movement in Italy, the regime installed by Dolfuss in Austria, Hitler's National Socialism, Franco's Falangism, Salazar's own version of order, the various eastern European systems (Beck's Poland, Horthy's Hungary, Antonescu's Rumania), Petain's Vichy regime, were marked by separate national traditions and differing political techniques, and they came to power in different circumstances. Nevertheless, they had certain traits in common. Firstly, they entailed forcible stabilization of existing property relationships. In each case, there was a threat of social revolution or at least of severe emendation of these relationships. A party opposed to these changes seized the state apparatus and used it to extirpate the opposition, to minimize or eliminate any political propaganda but its own, and to police the possibilities for the emergence of any new forms of oppositional activity. Secondly, these regimes had their own definitions of national community, which were enforced ideologically and culturally; they often had overtones of movements of national renaissance. The new national community was intended, indeed, to provide surcease from an excess of divisive internal social conflicts. Fascism in this respect was and is an effort to suppress the pattern of conflict in modern societies, not by eliminating many of its sources in the division of property but by controlling their political consequences. It is clear that on both counts a great amount of violence had to be used. It is clear that not all the regimes I have cited developed in industrial societies, and indeed one specific aspect of fascism in some historical circumstances has been a revolt of nonindustrial strata (peasants, and to some extent even the German educated) against the negative consequences industrialization entailed for these strata, economically and psychologically. A third aspect of the fascist systems is the aspect of national mobilization, closely connected with the notion of new national community (or of old community rediscovered or re-established). This often had to do with revanchist or imperialist ambitions.

It seems appropriate at this point to turn to the question of warfare and its political consequences for industrial society. Enough has been said, however, on the score of fascism to suggest that internal violence as a means of political control is perfectly compatible with an industrial order. Indeed, Americans aware of a certain strain of vigilantism in their national local political practice, aware too of the violence endemic to the maintenance of the supremacy of the white community, historically conscious of the xenophobia and chauvinism which are also parts of the heritage of a nation of immigrants (and often practiced precisely by recently established immigrant groups), and able to draw conclusions about the recent political successes associated with militant anti-Communism under the rubric "McCarthyism" will not be sure that under certain circumstances (a lost war or its foreign political equivalent, a breakdown or severe diminution in prosperity, or a prolonged and violent racial conflict) their own society will continue immune.

Warfare and preparation for warfare may or may not constitute the health of the state. In industrial societies, these impose upon the state and upon political elites indispensable tasks of centralization and direction. Part of the origins of modern bureaucratic states will be found in the early modern state's requirements for the maintenance of large standing military forces: the France of Louis XIV and Prussia were exemplary in this regard. The concern of enlightened monarchs for the welfare of their subjects was often a concern with a healthy and reasonably intelligent soldiery: again, the fact that Prussia had the first national system of elementary education in Europe is connected with its militarism. In general, warfare and preparation for it demand a rationalization of resources, heightened state intervention in the economy, and efforts to increase social cohesion. A certain contradiction has been evident historically. The military elites of western Europe were traditionally bound to aristocratic and, often enough, landed elements. Modern industrial warfare has required in addition to the conventional military virtues (authority, persistence, and courage) technical capacities of a quite different sort. Some of the sources of Prussia's and later Imperial and Nazi Germany's military efficacy may be found in the assimilation, in times of war, by the traditional military elite of educated administrators and technicians from the state bureaucracy and industry. That these were in turn influenced by *étatiste* conceptions tinged with military modes of organization made assimilation easier. In general, we may say that the enlarged role of the state in time of war has never been entirely undone in times of peace—not least in the liberal societies like Britain and America which are not customarily described in terms reserved for the more bureaucratic state systems.

Analyses of the state which rest on the institutionalization of violence as the critical factor in its functioning are usually opposed by analyses which insist on the role of consensus in the maintenance of the modern state. Indeed, there exists a considerable body of sociological thought which takes as its point of departure the gradual development of total consensus in the industrial societies, arguing that mature or modern societies are precisely those which include all of their adult members in a voluntary adherence to the social and political order. There is something curious about this position, but we would do best to first consider its strengths.

It is true that enlarged political participation, the consequence of the extension of suffrage, of popular political organization (especially for the working class), and of increases in the level of education and of affluence, has characterized industrial societies. Men, it can be argued, are no longer subjects; they have become citizens. Nations which were aggregations or conglomerates of populations living in moral as well as spatial dispersion have become communities. Indeed, the attenuation of local ties, the general phenomenon of social mobility characteristic of the industrial epoch, has resulted in a transformation of the notion of community. It is the modern nation-state which is now the privileged form of community, and nations may be regarded as successful only when their members are convinced that they do indeed belong to a community. It can be seen that there are two aspects to the argument. One deals with objective forms of political participation, the other with subjective sentiments—sentiments elaborated into ideological systems which of course possess objective characteristics of their own, and which are omnipresent elements in the life of nations.

The existence of consensus is more than an appearance, more than an epiphenomenon. Yet we do have to examine the texture of consensus and its many functions before we can say anything general about the extraordinarily varied historical forms it has assumed. We may begin by reminding ourselves that political participation, for most citizens of even nominally democratic nations, is highly infrequent. Enmeshed in the immediate concerns of their private lives, above all in the struggle for material existence, ordinary persons generally limit their politics to acts of compliance, indistinguishable from a pervasive acceptance of routine. Indeed, in societies characterized by an extreme division of labor, with distinct political structures, routine and compliance are the usual sources of consensus. Briefly, most persons do what they have to do without reflecting about it. The extent to which the exercise of power requires not a cowed or compliant populace, but one which accepts a specific complex of political beliefs, has been exaggerated. We may suppose that in the interstices of industrial society, a certain amount of political compliance comes not from adherence to an explicit set of ideas about the state, but from the factual interdependence and interpenetration of institutions which impinge directly upon the individual with those which may be somewhat more remote. Latin clericalism and anticlericalism both were rooted in strong local groupings, in the one case the parish, in the other a counter-community of secularists—in republican France concentrated in the public educational system. The history of France is evidence for the persistence of these local communities, despite was happening at the center of the state. The extent to which factory discipline, and in our own period the discipline of bureaucratic routine, has induced general attitudes of political compliance is very great. The factory, of course, has been the classical locale for the generation of revolutionary dispositions generalized to politics from their original focus on immediate sources of discontent. It is interesting, however, to note the sequence through which working-class discontent has passed. The first generation of revolutionary workers were often literate ex-artisans, quite capable themselves of thinking (with the aid of an intellectual culture they possessed to some extent) about the sources of their condition. The next generation was no less turbulent and no less of a threat to the structure of property. They directed their antagonism, however, more to factory owners than to the total organization of power in their societies; in time, the improved conditions of their daily material life reinforced the political concessions granted to the working class movement in diminishing its total and explicit refusal of the political order. The third phase, that of the integration of the working class in the political community, may now be upon us. If so, we are entitled to suppose that there is a connection between the greatly heightened work discipline and skill required in the modern production system and the assumption by the working class of what has been termed citizenship. We would do well to consider, in this respect, not only the possibilities of voluntary integration inherent in the current system but its capacity for covert suppression. It may be argued that a disciplined and skilled labor force has to be given full political equality, else discipline and skill will prove impossible to sustain. It can also be argued that inequality of access to culture, physical and moral absorption in the production line, and a general conditioning to a modern form of hierarchy combine to produce political compliance. The degree of conscious political consent required of the modern working class, in other words, is not necessarily very large: routine may be counted upon to do what is needed, and the essential aspect of routine is the acceptance of hierarchy at the workplace. Acceptance of hierarchy is even more pronounced for those in the middle class, or bourgeoisie, in administrative and professional occupations. Their very careers entail not only acceptance of hierarchy but factual complicity in its maintenance, in the actual exercise of power.

The search for the roots of consensus need not cause us to overlook the obvious. The tangible presence of a political order seems proof, at once, of its immutability and legitimacy. Even where its legitimacy is challenged, its sheer facticity can in the end prove overwhelming. Much has been made, with some reason, of the ways in which German national sentiment undermined the revolutionary ideology of German Social Democracy. That movement certainly proclaimed revolutionary goals, but the workers adhering to it passed through state schools, accepted factory discipline, served in the army, and benefited from social security legislation. In effect, the experience of integration in a national society confirmed an ideology explicitly rejected by the most articulate representatives of the German working class. Latent nationalist predispositions amongst the workers were important, but it was their daily routine which activated these.

Historically, a condition which resembles consensus may be the result of precisely its opposite, of the conflict of quite opposed definitions of national community. The changes which have taken place since the seventeenth century in the very notion of national community, the emergence of the idea of a public and a public good, have reflected the struggle of the bourgeoisie to supersede the absolutistic elites in command of the state. These claimed legitimation not from any conception of the public good but from theological imperatives, transmuted into the doctrine of divine right. The first major modern theorist to use the term consensus was Auguste Comte, as part of an effort to find a secular source of legitimation for political order within the boundaries of that order itself. Consensus was the condition of social stability, a result of the ideological and psychological consonance of familial and political authority. Comte's depiction of consensus was quite explicitly intended to show how society could be reintegrated after the ravages of the French Revolution and the subsequent reaction to it. The origins of the notion of consensus as a sociological concept, then, will be found in a nineteenth-century effort to overcome ideologies which divided society. Comte's recourse to unreflected adherence to authority, to the family, emphasized the social and psychological mechanisms producing sheer compliance. Characteristically, he proposed that ideological reflection—or rather, ideological indoctrination—become the task of an elite of specialists, exclusively empowered to deal with these questions. Comte's exegetes have been quick to find in this a secular imitation, or caricature, of the medieval church. Comte was, however, not alone in his effort to find surcease from modern ideological conflicts. Positivist and metaphysician, liberal and traditionalist, revolutionary socialist and defender of the bourgeois order, have since the French Revolution constituted so many ideological parties—each trying to capture the state and to monopolize the means of ideological production. So far from being organized about agreed systems of political beliefs, then, industrial societies have been arenas for ideological conflict. The struggle for consensus has been less a struggle to convert populations to given beliefs and more a struggle for command of the apparatus which would ensure if not acceptance of certain beliefs at least compliance with their institutional consequences.

When we do examine characteristic national definitions of political community, we find that what is most characteristic about them is the way in which they are not unified. The tradition of the French Revolution has been refused by the French right; not only the anti-Dreyfusards but the Vichyites espoused an alternative view of national history and politics. Meanwhile, those who adhered to the revolutionary tradition did so with differing interpretations of its implications: the French *petite bourgeoisie* in its obsession with small property and the socialist movement were frequently allies but often bitter enemies. They shared a common rhetoric, and this fact is perhaps a key to the forms of consensus in certain nations: ideological reflections of political conflicts occur in a single framework which sets the terms of the dispute. There are other instances, however, in which a publicly acknowledged framework and an implicitly held one of a different kind together constitute a form of consensual schizophrenia in the body politic. The egalitarianism and universalism which is so prominent an element in the official versions of the American consensus has always had to contend with a powerful underground stream of nativism. The current crisis in race relations in the United States suggests that the officially promulgated consensus is not unequivocally dominant. In Britain, a certain liberalism in the self-definition of the political community has been mixed with an important, if not always explicit, component of tribalism. These two have at times fused in the view that British liberalism is the product of a peculiar national genius and therefore inaccessible to other, lesser peoples. As for Germany, much of the current discussion of identity and identity crisis could be applied with some plausibility to that society's continuing and desperate search for a national idea. Recent developments suggest that the familiar combination of vulgar pan-Germanism and advanced technological and bureaucratic organization, despite consequences murderous for Europe and suicidal for Germany, is still not entirely without its appeal. Meanwhile, in the German Communist state, a Prussian ideal of national service in disrepair in western Germany lives on, in relatively easy co-existence with a rather special version of Marxism. In each of these societies, whatever forms of consensus may have attained a tenuous existence have been challenged by influential, not to say vocal, groups amongst the young. It is clear that industrial societies are perfectly able to function with enormous amounts of what I would term "dissensus": the question of power can by no means be answered by reference to consensus.

I have discussed consensus as the result of a more or less conscious adherence to certain beliefs about the political community. In the usual analysis of consensus, those participating in it identify their own national communities as repositories of objectively valid ideas of political order, and can then in good conscience perform their assigned social tasks. Above all, they can accept the authorities set above them. This analysis generally ignores the question, what causes men to espouse such beliefs? Suppose, for instance, that they are ignorant, or blind, or misled. The question, of course, assumes an ultimate human capacity to attain the truth, or a condition of spiritual maturity expressed in a community of sovereign members. It is, clearly, a modern question—one which reflects the ideals of the Enlightenment, and liberalism's critique of doctrines of the unreflecting nature of political order. One of this century's great cultural shocks, already anticipated by the more prescient in the last one, has been this: the spread of education and literacy, the experience of self-government, has not in fact made men more sovereign. The unreflecting consensus of traditional political orders, in which a majority of men could not read and had but crude conceptions of matters outside their immediate ken, has been replaced by a manipulated consensus. Those who think, in other words, have thoughts other than their own. The control of access to information, the control of the main media of communication, the command of the system of education, allow those who dominate the political order to impose their ideological will upon an intellectually inert population. How often, in industrial societies, does one hear ordinary persons repeating as if they were their own the most inspid, the crudest of clichés derived from the channels of mass communication. Moreover, in presenting the world as it is, in suppressing the possibility of critical thought (a suppression itself hardly conscious), the channels of mass communication generally reinforce that political compliance produced by routine. As I write these lines, a group of German students have taken to the streets to demonstrate their antagonism to the Springer Press, a newspaper trust which holds some 60 per cent of the West German press. The Springer newspapers may be described, in general, as bestial in their intellectual and moral level: the students, not without reason, consider this monopoly an obstacle to the democratization of German society, and it is difficult to disagree with the motto on many of their lapel buttons: "Bildlesen macht dumm." ("Reading *Bild* makes you stupid"—*Bild* in German for "picture" or "photograph," the name of the newspaper in question being, in effect, *Photo-News*.) The students have acted in terms of the theory of manipulated consensus. The populace, which has reacted with consternation and hostility to their protest, has by its comportment verified the theory. What they object to is that the students have disturbed their peace of mind, a tranquillity attained by renouncing all possibilities of thought other than those legitimated by being fixed in the media.

It may be objected that this view overlooks the considerable effectiveness of a certain pluralism in industrial societies. Industrial societies are stratified not least in terms of educational level, and the more educated may well entertain ideas more critical than those totally immersed in more mechanical routines. Even the stratification of the industrial population in terms of educational level, it may be said, subserves the maintenance of order. It is perhaps inevitable that many, trained for indispensable administrative and technical functions in the society, will know too much—or at least, think too much—about the incapacities of those with power. Those with critical or dissenting views are hindered from giving effective expression to them by two factors: (1) Their ability to communicate, culturally, with the rest of the population (which may well have latent or active discontents of its own) is limited by virtue of educational stratification. (2) Their occupational situation may oblige them to swallow their criticism, or isolate it from their routine services to those in power.

Nevertheless, it is true that dissensus and a certain amount of pluralism look alike. Indeed, we may say that some thinkers have mistaken a situation of dissensus for one in which there are pluralistic interpretations of consensually agreed conceptions of a political order. In fact, men accept political commands in most cases because they have no other alternatives.

This has been a somewhat lengthy excursus on violence, consensus, and dissensus—discussed as a mode of answering the question of the relationship of the modern state to industrial society. I have chosen to introduce these issues since so much political sociology rests on unacknowledged assumptions drawn from political philosophy, so much observation and analysis, in other words, is infused with a set of preferences as to the true or right political order. The analysis of the structural integration of the state with society will take a different form, depending upon the assumptions which underlie it. My own by this time are perfectly clear: we may now proceed to the substance of the matter.

III

The theoretic question is to what extent the modern state is relatively independent of the interest and power groupings in the larger society, to what extent its workings may be understood as the reflex of their activities. A general assertion will introduce the discussion: like its predecessors since the emergence of the modern national state, the industrial state not only has the negative if indispensable function of ensuring order by the violent repression of severe dissent, it has the positive function of adjucating and co-ordinating the workings of society. This function gives the state itself an interest in the maximization of its own capacity to intervene in social conflict. The state, it may be objected, is no monolithic entity. It is an historically variable complex of legislators and administrators, governments and their subjects, laws and their executants, formal prescriptions and unwritten but effective conventions. The question, then, can best be answered by some specific observations on the functioning of the modern state.

What gives the appearance of consensus to the modern state is its role as a mechanism for the allocation of property, for the ultimate control of the processes of production and distribution. The description of the modern state as a welfare state is a result of a certain confusion of two of its functions. In the first place, it guarantees property and constitutes the infra-structure for production and distribution. In the second (a far more restricted aspect of its operations), it actually assures the production of certain services like education, scientific research, and the maintenance of health, and also attempts a minimal distribution not of property but of income through channels like social security systems. The first function is far more important, quantitatively, than the second: the productivity of the modern economy is such that the substance of welfare is more likely to derive from full employment than from such income distribution as the state effects.

One of the striking features of the property and production maintenance functions of the state is its alliance, often to the point of interpenetration and infiltration, with those in command of property and the productive process. This relationship takes several forms. Those with interests to defend, or extend, may ally themselves directly with legislators and governments; they may concentrate their efforts on collaborating with (and not infrequently infiltrating) regulatory bureaucracies. Alternatively, or additionally, they may seek to influence opinion and the electorate (where there is one) to bring pressure upon legislators and governments. Concentrations of economic interest outside the state are relatively fixed and can operate on long-term schedules; this gives them certain advantages relative to varying political combinations of shorter effective duration. The state as spokesman for a (hypothetical) general interest, a public, is frequently at a disadvantage with respect to the persistent and specific pressures of large-scale property—nowhere more so than in the United States, where an ideology of individualism has been confounded with the workings of a highly organized market system, and where a negative connotation still attaches, for millions, to the idea of state intervention against property on behalf of the public good. More precisely, the public good is defined as requiring that the state refrain from curtailing the activities of those in command of large-scale property—and often defined so by those who have nothing but small-scale property and who are themselves exploited by those in command of the larger kind. It is here, perhaps, that the previous discussion of manipulated consensus may seem less hypothetical. At any rate, the evidence from a number of industrialized societies suggests that the political power of organized capital, however expressed, remains very great. The misadventures of the Labour Party, the innocuous behavior of the German Social Democrats in office, the utter inability of the Italian center-left coalition to undertake structural reforms, the difficulties of the Gaulist technocrats with the direction of a private sector traditionally reluctant to rationalize or take risks, constitute so much recent evidence for the ability of large-scale property holders (or managers) if not to impose their will upon the state at least to block or severely limit programs adverse to their interests. The present inability of the United States to cope with its urban problems is another, if somewhat more indirect, verification for the thesis. It is clearly in the interest of American capitalism to convert forty million paupers into forty million new customers; a program of urban reconstruction would on any reckoning provide an important stimulus to business. American political habitudes and American political structures, however, combine to make a government-directed program—however rational and imperative —an object of profound suspicion. These habitudes rest on a carefully cultivated ideology of "free enterprise" and on a factual collaboration of government with capital, mainly in the interest (if often long-term, as in the regulation of markets and the provision of an economic-political infrastructure) of the latter. The co-ordination necessary for urban reconstruction can come, apparently, only from government—but American capital has until now been reluctant to allow the government to co-ordinate outside the spheres of foreign and military affairs and those services which, however indispensable, were not profitable.

Several sorts of objection have been raised to this sort of argument. The first concerns the political representation of the organized working class and of social groups not identical with the proprietors of large-scale property. It is certainly true that there has been a secular trend for increased integration of the organized working class in national political systems: the slow but irreversible evolution to "reformism" of the French and Italian Communist parties reflects their recognition of this tendency. The secular trend, however, has not been uninterrupted: in addition to continual cyclical movements in the economy which socialist as well as bourgeois governments have been unable to check, there have been long periods of repression directed against the organized working class. Fascism, understood in one of its aspects as the forcible stabilization of property relationships, is less than a generation distant in western Europe. Moreover, and more importantly, the integration of the working class in national political systems has not altered their stratified, or class, character. Integration has served to blunt the cutting edge of working-class militancy, to canalize it into partial if direct conflicts with property, but it has not produced notably more egalitarian societies. Such new egalitarianism as we may establish is as much the result of secular increases in the productivity of the economy as in changes in the control of production or redistribution of income. The second, related objection refers directly to the institutions of public welfare. These, with medical insurance, unemployment benefits, and retirement insurance, have surely diminished the inhumanities of total market systems. It is sometimes overlooked, however, that the state mechanisms and institutions developed for these purposes have effected a redistribution of the working class's own income. Forced saving and deferred income, the shifting of burdens from one segment of the working class to another, the utilization of a share of capital which might otherwise have been subject to direct attack by unions or socialist parties (and which enterprise has been able to amortize as labor cost), are among the devices employed. In the end, the working class (and the populace generally) has paid for its own social benefits. In general, it may be said that rationalized welfare systems entail the assumption by the state of responsibility for a relatively disciplined and productive labor force. It is difficult, upon reflection, to see this as an attack on the efficacy of large-scale property.

The most telling argument about the new character of the industrial state is a different one. There exists, we are told, an increasingly large and increasingly powerful group of political technicians with experience and expertise in a set of disciplines indispensable to the functioning of the modern state: law and administration, economics and finance, science and technology, urbanism and health, military and political affairs. These technicians monopolize competence and experience in these fields: ordinary politicians and parliamentarians, except in the cases in which they themselves are recruited from amongst the technicians, may nominally exercise authority over the technicians, but in fact the latter can and do frame policy. They control information, so that their advice on the formulation of policy generally amounts to policy formulation itself. As policy executants, they enjoy such latitude in the conduct of government that they exercise political functions. Indeed, so indispensable are these men to the direction of the modern state that they have begun to move into the political parties and governments: a new type of politician is emerging, particularly in the United States. Where, as in western Europe, educated technicians have always been prominent in politics, the educational qualifications of the group have begun to change. Lawyers are no longer as important as they were, and economists and technologists have become more prominent.

The increasing political importance of the state technicians is, of course, a consequence of late developments in the process of bureaucratization. Ever more spheres of social life have been subjected to rationalization by hierarchical administrative structures. In these explicit criteria of competence, educational qualifications and administrative and technical expertise govern rank. The modern national state, the successor to the Roman Church as the co-ordinating institution of modern society, was the progenitor of bureaucracy—which then spread to industrial production and economic administration. The demise of

the liberal state, the attenuation of purely juridical qualifications for office in the centralized state systems, has accounted for a revivification of bureaucratic political technique in the contemporary state. (Witness the application
of what are termed "modern management methods" in the
American federal departments, most visible recently in
MacNamara's reign at the Department of Defense.)
Bureaucratic technique in this setting, however, is more
than the static administration of a nationl patrimony,
the execution of tasks assigned by a political directorate,
the assimilation of new problems to old, mainly legal categories. It is the rationalization of political choice itself,
the desacralization of politics, the treatment of social conflict as matter for technical manipulation. The system apparently lends itself well to forms of democracy which are
virtually plebiscitary in parliamentary guise of one or another sort. The electorate designates a set of leaders on the
basis of an exceedingly general program, and the winning
team seeks the means to realize these general ends. No recent political process is more obvious; none has been so
much discussed; none has been subject to such misinterpre-
tation.

In the first instance, this development has given rise to
the familiar thesis of "the end of ideology," promulgated
in its recent form by Raymond Aron and adopted for
American use by Daniel Bell. Utopian and radical demands for the reconstruction of society, it is argued, no
longer move either industrial populations or any considerable section of their intellectual elites. Instead, the profane challenge of a succession of concrete problems within
a relatively stable social order has come to dominate political consciousness. In the circumstances, political and social
technique has become more important than new social
ideas, political and social technicians are more honored

(and infinitely more effective) than politicians weighted by ideological ballast. Karl Popper's celebrated prescription for "piecemeal social engineering" is a rhetorically different expression of the same thesis. I shall deal shortly with some of the general implications of the thesis for our view of the institutionalization of power in industrial society. For the moment, let us consider the question of the political technician's autonomy of decision, implied by the notion of a politics devoid of ideology. It is difficult to suppose, upon reflection, that the technicians are totally devoid of ideology—however unreflected or unarticulated their ideology or ideologies may be. The criterion of technical efficacy is in itself an ideology, and often enough one curiously insensitive to its potential for conflict with other sets of value. It is more than the ideology of a technocratic elite, although it is frequently that; it is also the end product, distorted, shrunken, and detached from its original and sometimes humane purposes, of the view that science and technology provide a canon for the mastery of society. The political technicians, moreover, are far from a self-contained group: they share social background, common educational experiences, perspectives, and often careers with men in the other bureaucratic systems of industrial society. Their class position, in other words, has a certain influence upon them—as do direct pressures from other groups. Finally, technical efficacy is in fact not an exclusive criterion of political decision: technical choices (including the choices of technical means) are permeated by political values. Precisely what political values (in themselves of course derivatives of ideologies) underlie the specific choices of the political technicians varies from case to case. In all cases, these depend upon the relationships of the apex of the state bureaucracy to the elites in command of the other great power groups. In practice, again, the state and organized property interpenetrate—even where coalition and conflict alternate.

The rise of the state technicians, then, does not mean the elimination of ideology from politics. The current debate on the sources of American poverty, with urbanists, economists, sociologists, psychologists, and a host of other experts at each other's throats, is evidence for the continuing ideologicization of politics. Arguments about the role of familial structure in engendering attitudes to work, about local or national control of poverty programs, about the incorporation of capitalist enterprise in an anti-poverty program (or about the incorporation of a program in the agenda of capitalist enterprise), about the role of an autonomous black population in state and society, are not simply technical differences. They call into play fundamental notions of social order, of the good society, and refract and express fundamental and conflicting social interests. The state technicians, here as elsewhere, exercise power.

The exercise of power by state technicians, however, is not identical with the domination of a society by a uniform elite of technocrats. That technicians have risen to directing posts in the economy, in public institutions (whether publicly administered or not) like educational systems and the media of communications, is clear. They subserve interests, however, other than their own; indeed, they frequently define their own interests (as I have just suggested above) in terms derived from their alliances with other groups. In particular, much has been made of the substitution of impersonal forms of corporate property for direct private ownership of the sort characteristic of industrial property in the early entrepreneurial epoch of capitalism. It follows, for some, that the managers of corporate property are in effect the civil servants of advanced capitalism. The analogy may be correct, but its exegesis allows a conclusion other than that of the existence of a technocratic elite uniform in its composition and monolithic in its politics. The property managers' interests are in the maintenance and extension of the privileges which accrue to property, and these often enough conflict with the interests served by the state technicians. That a long-term balance of power may align the two, in certain societies (certainly in the United States up to now) does not exclude short-term conflicts or differences. Furthermore, that the technocrats constitute an elite element in a society and a political system increasingly technicized does not render them spokesmen for the intermediate sectors of the technical intelligentsia: the interests of the engineers who work for a large corporation and of those with engineering degrees who sit on its board of directors or occupy its executive posts continue to differ. Quite apart from their relationships within the boundaries of the enterprise itself, these groups may pursue political interests (with respect to fiscal policy, government expenditure on social services, and even foreign policy) of a quite different kind. We are still obliged to understand industrial politics as the interpenetration of state and property systems.

For the United States (as for Imperial Britain before it), property and state systems coalesce most obviously in the conduct of foreign affairs. Foreign affairs, in the industrial epoch, include far more than relationships between sovereign states: they encompass investment abroad, the exercise of political and economic influence in other countries by agencies other than governmental ones, the covert intervention in the affairs of other nations effected by clandestine official agencies, and ostensibly nonpolitical cultural activities. (It will be recalled that the American Central Intelligence Agency financed a cultural organization which had the effrontery to use these funds to establish "independent" journals in a number of countries, all of them extolling the virtues of political pluralism.) Domestic spending for the varied activities categorized as "defense" and overseas investment constitute important components of the American economy: state and economy are nowhere so intertwined as in these spheres. The frequent movement of technicians and politicians (if the two categories can be kept apart) between posts in the state agencies dealing with foreign affairs and the private sector have reinforced a similarity of perspective *re* conventional definitions of the national interest. The description by a prominent social critic of anti-Communism as a racket may well apply to certain intellectuals; as far as the private sector is concerned, it is good business. The enormous resources at the direct disposition of the state in these spheres, the inertial force of certain policies (anti-Communism has been more quickly modified by the American elites than by a public indoctrinated over decades), the necessity for delegating authority to the state in times of crisis, do combine to endow the state with a very considerable short-term autonomy in the conduct of foreign affairs. That there is a long-term consonance of state and property interests in the conduct of foreign policy seems clear. What is less clear is the extent to which certain features of America's intenal politics can be attributed to this consonance. Here, an enumeration may be helpful. Manpower is planned (through mechanisms like government educational policies and the workings of Selective Service) with a view toward strengthening the nation in international competition; economic policies and social investment generally are adjusted to "defense" spending (consider the enormous stupidity of the moon race, with its distorting effect on the entire nation's technological resources);

above all, the limits of national consensus have been set at those compatible with a rapid psychological mobilization of the population in the defense of a schematic notion of the national interest.

America's young (and old) radicals consider the adventure in Vietnam more than a miscalculation or a mistake; they think of it as the supreme expression of a polity organized internally for external repression. The recent popular revulsion for the war, and its electoral consequences, would seem to refute them; at the very least, we may say that the internal consensus on violent anti-Communism is not immovable. Before reaching our final judgment, however, we would do well to note that this popular revulsion followed and did not precede a considerable current of doubt and disillusionment about the war amongst political and economic elites. These elites have utilized their command positions in the foreign policy apparatus to legitimate themselves as servitors of the national interest: the distinction between its own interests and those of these elites, with respect to foreign affairs, has proven up to now practically impossible for the populace to make.

It is true that considerable economic benefits accrued ɔ a good proportion of the entire population as a resɪ ɪ of American foreign relations. In this connection, it is suggestive that the rhetoric of the two Kennedy brothers, their insistence that only a more equitably organized American society can effectively prosecute a global mission, represents an enlightened version of American imperialism. As the examples of Bismarck's Germany and Lloyd George's Britain showed, an enlightened imperialism remains imperialism. At any rate, the sphere of foreign affairs is precisely the sphere in which the interpenetration of state and property seems to have advanced the furthest; it remains to be seen what role property will play in the new fields of gigantic state intervention in America—education, health and welfare services, and urbanism. The preliminary evidence suggests that corporate enterprise envisages a certain collaboration with the state in these areas, possibly involving the nationalization of risk, but certainly involving corporate profit.

National differences are important. I have already referred to the difference in political tradition between the liberal state and the centralized or bureaucratic one. The degree to which organized property can dominate the state is also a consequence of the explicit resistance to property by other interest groups. Where the organized working class can delegate to parliaments, through working-class parties, its own representatives we may witness counterpressure on the state technicians. The acceptance by working-class parties of reformist or ameliorative goals as a long-range program, however, inclines these representatives to collaboration with organized property in the state apparatus itself. The recent parliamentary debates on the French five-year plan were instructive in this respect. The protests of disfavored regions, of a working class disadvantaged by loss of possible social investments (in education and welfare, in cultural facilities and transport) out to relieve the tax burden on industry, were extremely vocal. On the actual plan commission, and in its subcommissions, practical compromises were effected. The French situation approaches one in which the state technicians nominally hold the balance of power. Their power has been strengthened by the state's capacity to manipulate lending rates for the private sector and by actual state participation in many enterprises. Nonetheless (a finding which would also apply to Italy with its large state sector), the plans and governmental economic policies generally have been far more responsive to the pressures and requirements of the private sector than to the demands and needs of the bulk of the working population. It must be said that the civil servants and political technicians involved (including someone like Michel Debré or François Bloch-Laine, Gaullist technicians par excellence) have often given a perfectly straightforward and plausible explanation for their policies: the strength of the nation, they argue, depends upon the vitality of the economy. In circumstances in which no structural changes in property relations of a dramatic kind are envisaged, it is the duty of the state to strengthen the productive apparatus; advantages for private property are either means to this end or incidental by-products of a policy which envisages the long-term public good. (I will add that I have heard not dissimilar arguments from a member of the Central Committee of the French Communist Party, a parliamentarian with good chances of becoming a minister in some subsequent Popular Front coalition: we are a party about to assume major responsibilities, he declared, and revolutionary rhetoric is irrelevant. It is interesting in this connection that the P.C.F. has turned its attention recently to broadening its electoral base: away from exclusive representation of the working class and intellectuals sympathetic to it, and toward the technical intelligentsia.) The force of current circumstances then, the necessity of making decisions within a given political and economic environment, incline the state technicians to collaboration with the private sector even in a situation in which the Jacobin state tradition and developed notions of *dirigisme* could have indicated different solutions.

The British case is somewhat different, again. Labor came to office in 1964 with an elaborate critique of the irrationalities and inefficiencies of British capitalism, as well as of its inequities. Indeed, Harold Wilson had called for a rejuvenation of capitalist management, with the slogan "no dead wood in the boardroom"—certainly a slogan not entirely revolutionary. In the end, Labour's domestic social programs and much of its scheme for industrial change were sacrificed to fiscal exigencies imposed on Britain by an alliance of foreign governments and international finance. The Labour politicians in office, many of them with experience of the civil service or of a higher civil service social background and mentality, have behaved like civil servants or state technicians and not like radical reformers or representatives of the working class. That is to say that the peculiar British state tradition, with its emphasis on the maintenance of consensus, inclines state technicians and technically minded politicians to extreme caution in dealing with property. That in this case the property involved was international appears to have strengthened caution.

The current German case is affected, of course, by the special historical circumstances of that unhappy nation. The Prussian tradition in the civil service appears to have gone, having been succeeded by pedantic legalism, political careerism, or (particularly with respect to defense procurement) outright corruption. The Social Democratic Party, which may be described as slightly reformist, might have been thought capable of introducing into government a new technical dimension; it has done so, to some extent, in certain model provinces where it has long been in office (Hesse and Berlin, for instance). Even this has been impeded on the federal level, despite the Party's acceptance of office, by other priorities. The Party took office for electoral reasons (to demonstrate its "respectability") and national ones (to make some progress toward an accommodation with the German Communist state). Policy remains the domain of an unreflected consensus, a direct expression—untransformed by any discernible tradition—of the current balance of power amongst the social classes and interest groups. In the circumstances, a technical rationalization of public administration seems difficult of attainment, and the Federal Republic appears to be a somewhat backward polity. That rationalization, insofar as it has been attempted (with new experiments in fiscal and budgetary planning, and in scientific and technological policy), has not resulted in an autonomous role for state technicians seems certain.

It remains to consider the political function of parliamentary institutions and, beyond that, of electoral systems. Parliamentary institutions are, in western industrial societies, now apparently firmly established. There is no necessary connection between industrialism and parliamentary government, however, and recent history has shown how tenuous they may be even in nations with democratic traditions. The emergence of the state technicians, the collaboration of state bureaucracies with the bureaucracies outside the state, or their pursuit of direct conflict with these bureaucracies with little regard for parliamentary bodies, the direct pressure of interest groups and social classes on governments and the consequent diminution of the mediating role of parliament, have all combined to reduce the efficacy of parliaments. State bureaucracies and their counterparts in the private sector can pursue long-term strategies; parliaments are relatively short-lived and individual parliamentarians may have discontinuous careers in office. Moreover, parliamentarians are peculiarly subject to the varying influences of propaganda campaigns in their own districts, persuasion by various means (including overt or covert corruption) by politically interested property concentrations, and manipulation by their own party leaders—especially when these occupy governmental posts and can distribute or withhold patronage. Strong and centralized party organization is not invariably a factor in increasing the independence of either individual parliamentarians (dependent upon the party for office, funds, and advancement) or of parliament as a whole (where both governmental and oppositional parties may be subjected to strenuous discipline). The bureaucratization of working-class parties (whether Social Democratic or Communist) has been notorious; their cohesiveness in the face of the superior political power of property and propertied groups has often been purchased, then, at the price of flexibility and spontaneity. It may well be that as geographical mobility increases in industrial nations, as social differentiation becomes a function less of regional divergences than of the contrasting economic position of the social classes, the local basis of parliamentary representation will become increasingly obsolete. "One man, one vote" remains a noble ideal. In any event the practical force of social differentiation is to deny this ideal in the practice of parliamentary systems. The attachment of many parliamentarians to sponsors of a socio-economic kind (including, of course, unions) perhaps indicates future parliamentary forms. The direct representation of unions, economic enterprises, and other corporate bodies may be as rational and as democratic a way to conduct parliamentary business as present forms—here, as elsewhere, French thought, and the beginnings of French practice are most advanced. The Jacobin technocrat, Mendès-France, has proposed a second chamber organized in this way, and the Economic Council with its regional commissions, working with the Plan Commission, already seems to be more important than the French Senate.

In the discussion of consensus, I have dealt with the nature of popular participation in politics in industrial societies. Except for crises which engender the formation of mass movements, that participation remains infrequent and often immensely superficial. The hyper-organization of bureaucratized societies has had a paradoxical result: the political atomization of industrial populations. The objection that atomization as a general condition is fictitious, since industrial societies know occupational or work groupings, ties of family and neighborhood, confessional organization, and a modicum of local community, is perhaps true—but politically irrelevant. These groupings are not foyers of direct political participation. Indeed, the divorce of life from politics in these settings is a major source of the political malaise of modern nations. These contexts offer direct contact with others, a certain transparency and predictability in the social environment. Politics seems remote and opaque, almost arcane. The frenzy of the fascist mentality in industrial societies seems to express a desperate effort to establish control over circumstances become both intolerable and inexplicable. Meanwhile, the movements of liberation in the socialist tradition have become increasingly ossified or authoritarian, sometimes both. That the liberal conception of an enlightened citizenry, of a public opinion, should retain any simulacrum of verity is in our circumstances more astonishing than the severe emendation in liberal hopes imposed on us by history. A future politics of liberation will have to work not only with formal notions of representation and legitimation, but with the intent of maximizing participation in a political process now largely monopolized by bureaucratic elites of one or another sort. What concrete programs this may entail remains to be seen. For the moment, we may say that if the age of ideology is indeed finished, it is not necessarily an occasion for satisfaction. A new industrial politics is, particularly in its beginnings, unlikely to be

free of visionary or utopian elements—but only new uto-
pias may suffice to apprehend the democratic possibilities
of a society increasingly dominated by science, technique,
and administration.

We encounter, here, the problem of the political avant-
garde in industrial politics. Our estimate of its historical
potential may be affected by our evaluation of an inchoate
but much more prominent countermovement: the political rear guard of industrial society. The unevenness of social development has everywhere left sizeable pockets of
resistance to the tendencies I have sketched above—retrograde and declining groupings unable to connect their own
experiences with the new production technology and administrative or bureaucratic politics, threatened by the dis-
location of their privileges and perspectives. Analyses of
electoral support for parties of the right, discussions of the
social composition of the European fascist movements,
the recent literature on the radical right in America, generally point to these popular sources of support: those outside the mainstream of advanced urban culture, traditionalist peasants, petty proprietors, marginal *rentiers,* groups
and strata imperiled by drastic and sudden deprivation
of their conventional status expectation. It is quite true
that a generalized socio-economic and political crisis is required to activate these discontents, that their political
mobilization frequently has occurred in coalition with
movements and ideologies which were not unequivocally
committed to the defense of property. The Nazi Party until 1934 had an influential left wing, and the state socialist
component in its program was not eradicated by its alliance with German capitalism. In circumstances of normal
socio-economic function industrial societies seem able to
encapsulate their retrograde elements, who also constitute
—alas—evidence for the persistent role of ignorance

and stupidity in politics. (Consider the inanities promulgated, and even believed, by the new American right.) The politics of those imperfectly incorporated in industrial society, then, constitute a constant threat to its delicate balance of force, situational constraint, and voluntary conformity. We may say that the retrograde, when activated, have given proof not alone of their stupidity but also of a certain stubbornness not devoid of exceedingly primitive insight. They have refused to accept the discrepancy between their own expectations and the real possibilities open to themselves. The hatreds and energies released by their refusal have frequently fixed on scapegoats and on delusionary programs. The very pathology of their demand for order and normalization (in the names of which they have sanctioned murder and extirpation) have served to expose the pathologies of their total historical setting. It is precisely at this point that the political avant-garde has begun its own critique of political reality.

The idea of a political avant-garde is, I will admit, highly imprecise. An avant-garde may be understood historically or temporally as a group of innovators pointing the way to developments as yet unrealized—or scarcely discernible—in culture and politics. It may be understood structurally as a group of dissenters experimenting with cultural and political forms inexpressible within the constraints of a specific system and, very possibly, incapable of institutionalization in any system. The early industrial vision of the political avant-garde was polarized: Saint-Simon spoke for (and about) an elite of engineers and entrepreneurs who would sweep away the detritus of the *ancien régime,* whereas the early socialists and Marx described the historical tasks awaiting the proletariat. It is difficult to consider engineers and entrepreneurs (now managers) as candidates for avant-garde status today, although the technical intelligentsia may be the repository of a radical potential as yet largely unmobilized. As for the proletariat, become the industrial working class, it is neither in its culture nor its politics a harbinger of the future or a revolutionary force. Today's avant-garde in industrial societies will be found amongst the young, particularly students (that is to say, those without immediate responsibilities or bondages to the existing order), and amongst intellectuals, those with a certain freedom from routine and a certain proclivity to employ their critical faculties.

The revolt of the students—supported, with some hesitations and ambivalences—by their elders amongst the intellectuals, is as international as it was (originally) surprising. Had not we read of the "found generation" in America, of the "sceptical generation" in Germany, of the "tranquilized" students in Gaullist France? Have we not also been told that repression combined with indoctrination effectively minimizes dissent in the state socialist societies (to which I shall turn shortly) and that in any case the students there are thoroughly de-ideologicized and interested in careers? The source of our surprise lay, perhaps, in the widespread acceptance enjoyed by the thesis of the end of ideology—it having been supposed that the (temporary or more enduring) loss of ideological enthusiasm by industrial populations would in the end induce intellectuals to abandon theirs. In any event, precisely the populace's reluctance to conceive of other possibilities of social existence has incited the students to constitute themselves as a political avant-garde. Faced with a society apparently able to reproduce itself indefinitely, with a material culture which seemingly smothered spiritual experience, with well-functioning social machinery requiring only new cogs, a surprisingly radicalized generation has responded by an extremely violent rejection of the whole.

It is quite true that these students are everywhere in the minority, amongst the many categories of students and the young generally, but they do include some of the liveliest and most intelligent members of the ascendant genera-tion. In America, they have sought and at times effected an alliance with the underclass. Elsewhere, in western Eu-rope, they have conceived of themselves as allied across in-ternational boundaries with the revolutionary movements of the Third World: Mao, Castro, Guevara, Fanon attract them, and Régis Debray is in a sense a representative of an entire European age group. The seeming abstractness and remoteness of this alliance contrasts with the concrete forms taken by generational politics in the turbulence that has beset the universities recently. Perhaps, however, the two tendencies are connected.

The ideology of the students insists on the surrogate role assumed by these bourgeois young people in a world still racked by exploitation. Working with southern Negroes and the northern poor, the American student avant-garde has helped end the illusion that their country was, at once, totally integrated and without a proletariat. They have expressed the bad (or good) conscience of their fathers. With respect to the global underclass in the Third World, the western students (at times in the absurd fashion de-picted by Godard in *La Chinoise*) have insisted on the ex-tension of the notions of political community to the rela-tions between exploitative and exploited peoples. It should not be forgotten that in France, the resistance to the Al-gerian war was for a long period led almost exclusively by the teachers' and university students' unions. In America, the resistance to the war in Vietnam began in the univer-sities. The students' and intellectuals' moral repudiation of the older and newer forms of imperialism has not yet been attached to any viable theory of a new politics. The bulk of the industrial population is indifferent, where not actively hostile, to their views on the Third World. (The wars in Algeria and Vietnam occasioned severe political divisions in the elite, and this is why the Algerian war ended and why the one in Vietnam may end, sooner or later.) I have said that the anti-imperialism of the student movement (and of its adult allies) is not attached to a politically viable theory. Perhaps it would be more accurate to say that it is not yet attached to one; it certainly derives from a more or less coherent view of the global role of industrial societies in their present stage of development. The present political efficacy of the student movement is limited; on the face of it, the movement constitutes a desperate, if continuing, guerilla action within an internally consolidated society. Potentially, however, the situation is different.

The students' critique of their own society and their refusal of the roles assigned to them in it constitutes an anticipatory strike by a critical segment of the labor force. In training for elite and sub-elite occupations, the students have repudiated the routine careers open to them—despite the very obvious rewards which would come from compliance with the requirements of the usual career sequences. Instead, they have insisted on the amoral or immoral quality of careerism, because implicated in a structure of domestic authoritarianism and global imperialism. Offered the chance to occupy the command posts of the technological society of the future, they have criticized the moral validity of the distinction between rulers and the ruled. Apprentice philosophers offered the chance to become kings, they have declared that true philosophy is incompatible with kingship. Within the universities, under the extremely general slogan of "student power," they have demanded a form of participatory democracy which would wrench the bureaucratic university from its position as an exemplary training center for a hierarchical society. Knowledge and technique, they declare, have other and more humane uses than those to which society now puts them. In the circumstances, we may ask if present student discontent might not (if in forms which will eventually disappear) represent the politics of the future technical intelligentsia. These politics would demand that those who have knowledge and technique participate in the total process of government and administration, not as mere technical specialists but as typical of an educated and self-governing citizenry. It has not occurred to the students that the demand for participation in the control of knowledge and technology, more precisely the demand for full control of the production and distribution of knowledge, could eventuate in a new technocratic elitism. For the moment, the demand is joined to a general critique of the undemocratic and repressive character of a technological society—attributed, variously, to its organization for imperialism and its failure to rationalize and enlarge democracy from a parliamentary form to a total social praxis. Whether the movement is the last expression of a socialist humanism which has taken final refuge in the universities, or whether it prefigures radical new political developments amongst the technical intelligentsia, we cannot yet say. For the moment, we may state that the political avantgarde in Western industrial societies is found amongst the students. The spectacles of the red flag mounted by 10,000 Sorbonne students on the Arc de Triomphe while the Communist Party gravely condemns "adventurism"; of German students attacking the printing factories of a reactionary press lord, to have the German Trade Unions Congress bar student spokesmen from its May Day rallies; of students seizing the campuses at Berkeley and Columbia with a prosperous American working class concerned about law, order, and property values—these suggest that late industrial society still contains profound contradictions, and perhaps important possibilities for political change.

IV

These essays concentrate on societies of which I have considerable direct experience: Britain, France, Germany and the United States. A scholar himself attached to the Marxist tradition and interested in relevance ought not to avoid dealing with the state socialist regimes of central and eastern Europe (China seems to present a special case, although the influence of Maoism in Europe certainly reflects the contradictions I have just mentioned). These regimes know state property only, administered with the ostensible goal of maximizing the public good. An essential element in their official ideology is the claim that the elimination of large-scale private property existing as an independent political entity renders the state socialist regimes truly democratic, representatives of the higher interests of the total community rather than agencies of exploitative forces within it.

An examination of this claim may illuminate some of those essential characteristics of the inner movement of industrial societies which are independent of the nature of their political regimes. Not quite paradoxically, it may also tell us something of the relationship between political regime and social structure in industrial circumstances.

There is no large-scale private property in the state socialist regimes, and therefore no managerial or propertied elite whose power and status derives from property. Large-scale state property does exist, and those who control it do

make decisions which directly affect the bulk of the population—decisions relative to the level and type of investment, hours of work and remuneration, the price of goods
and services. The elite in command of state property also
commands the state, which in these regimes has fused po-
litico-economic functions. It is the ruling party which staffs
the bureaucratic hierarchies of state and economy and
which centralizes decision at their intersecting apexes. The
economic interests pursued by the party are nominally
(and possibly actually) those dictated by the long-term
interests of the nation. Despite the promise of the socialist
tradition, however, the nation has no direct means of controlling the processes of production and distribution.
Syndicalist and other forms of popular participation in the
direction of the economy, with the conspicuous exception
of Yugoslavia, are missing. The extraction of surplus value
from the population for its own long-term benefit (or the
benefit of its descendants) clearly differs in intent and
consequence from the extraction of surplus value on behalf
of the propertied. The calculus of benefit, however, does
not fall to the population but to the elite in control
of property—an elite which in the course of administering
the national economic patrimony has also secured considerable advantages for itself.

The state socialist nations are no less stratified than the
capitalist ones. The conjoined economic and political
power of the ruling party makes high party position a
guarantor of power and status in the nation; the insistence
of the party on direct control of the economic system has
attested the importance of control of property in the maintenance of party power. We need not think of the party as
a force outside the economic system: it is deeply immersed
in it. Indeed, what is at issue is less the existence of a repressive political apparatus alone than the utilization of

that apparatus to maintain a system of stratification, to which the term "class system" may be attached with no very great difficulty. .(The state socialist elite has been able to transmit the advantages of its own position to its offspring, through its explicit and implicit control of access to the educational system.)

Direct political control in the state socialist regimes has entailed repression and manipulation, combining or alternating in dreadful periodicity. Repression has taken the form of the prohibition on all political activity apart from that conducted by the party (or by certain captive parties in the coalition regimes of eastern and central Europe); of a strict control of the media of communication; and, of course, of terror. Manipulation (now more prominent than terror) has consisted of indoctrination through the utilization of selective images of social and political reality; the alternation of economic punishment and reward for political compliance; the ideological and social fragmentation of the bases on which oppositional groups could coalesce.

How does this schematic depiction of the reality of the state socialist regimes relate to the centrifugal phenomena which are now apparent in them? We may use their centrifugality precisely to deepen our understanding of their inner movement. In the first instance, I have spoken of a uniform party elite. The recent emergence (or re-emergence, since the same conflicts were visible, for example, in the Soviet Union in the 1920's) of divisions between political functionaries and industrial managers has not necessarily constituted a threat to party rule. Rather, it has entailed conflicts within the party by groups pursuing different versions of the general interest as well, of course, as their own. It is clear that industrial managers (recruited from those with technical educations) will insist on economic criteria for economic decisions, while those with more political viewpoints will insist on the primacy of other policy considerations. To this must be joined the interest of the generalists and ideologues in the party in the retention of a dominant position in the party apparatus, the interest of the managers (and of the technicians generally) in the recognition of their special responsibilities. The balance seems to be altering in favor of the latter.

Meanwhile, in the interstices of the state and the economy and in the system of cultural production, new and (sometimes oppositional) tendencies have developed. A technical intelligentsia conscious of its social importance and aware of its increasing size has begun to demand the application of technical criteria of competence in the management of state and economy. This by no means entails a threat of the reversal of the regime; rather, it implies the accentuation of the technocratic elitism within it. From the dictatorship of the party (in the name of the proletariat) to the concentration of power in the hands of the technicians (in the name of the nation) is not, after all, an impossibly giant step. The restlessness of the intellectuals engaged in the more abstract or symbolic forms of cultural production (literature and pure science) has, at times, assumed more overtly oppositional forms. A protest at rigid and dogmatic party cultural control has been broadened into a critique of the quality of life, the possibilities of expression, under the state socialist regimes. The critics, open to cultural and political influence from other social systems, have been especially susceptible to arguments derived from the utopian aspects of Communist doctrine: the revolution's present reality has been measured against its early promise, and found entirely wanting.

The possible success of these groups in modifying the structures of state socialism inherited from the Stalinist epoch will depend upon their abilities to mobilize a significant body of public opinion behind themselves. Public opinion, in the state socialist regimes, has become increasingly less ephemeral. With the relaxation of total terror, the informal channels of communication (at the workplace and in the home) have opened: an unofficial public opinion, with a critical content strikingly different from that conveyed by the official media, has begun to crystallize. It has thus far focused on two issues: immediate economic conditions, and what we may term national sentiment. This last has been especially pronounced in those regimes established in eastern and central Europe after the war by Soviet occupation. It has most recently been used by retrograde elements in certain parties to resist demands for liberalization made by the intellectuals, denounced as excessively cosmopolitan (or Jewish). In general, one of the most interesting recent developments in the state socialist countries has been the increasing appeal of contending party factions to public opinion. The spectacle of a discredited party boss in Czechoslovakia (Novotny) appealing to the "good sense" of the workers against his intellectual critics was repulsive; it contained within it, however, possibilities for an enlargement of the debate which eventually swept Novotny from office.

The ultimate questions with respect to public opinion are two. In economies no less technological than those in the capitalist societies and no less dependent upon an increasingly skilled labor force, the maintenance of a relatively primitive system of ideological tutelage by a single party may not be compatible with the attainment by the population of the educational levels required by the administrative and productive apparatus. (The revolt of the students, it will be recalled, has extended across both sides of the ideological boundary dividing the capitalist and state socialist sectors of industrial society.) Secondly, the state socialist regimes (again with the exception of Yugoslavia) have as yet to develop direct mechanisms for the expression of public opinion. Intraparty democracy is hardly developed in any formal sense, much less an authentic multiparty system; the media of communication are still the exclusive property of the party; the trade unions are almost invariably docile. Events in the spring of 1968 in Czechoslovakia—a nation with a democratic tradition, missing elsewhere in eastern and central Europe—suggest that an astonishing experiment in the democratization of state socialism has been launched, with what ultimate results it is at this writing impossible to tell.

This brief attempt to describe the state socialist regimes does allow some general conclusions. The interpenetration of state and economy in these regimes has resulted in the relative decline of a purely political leadership; power now seems to be shifting (if slowly) to men with technical qualifications, able to work out the technical implications of political decisions and increasingly demanding a voice in the latter. The technicians are not detached from state property; they are, instead, its immediate controllers. The state socialist regimes allow us to envisage a development which seems universal: in the highly technical and fused administrative and productive systems which constitute industrial societies, the notion of "pure" property (whether corporate property of the capitalist sort or state property of the state socialist kind) is obsolete. The range of activity connected with property maintenance (or production) has constantly widened. A narrow Stalinist party elite insisted on increasing the powers of the productive apparatus; to serve that apparatus in its contemporary phase, a new technical elite and a technical intelligentsia subordinate to it has begun to challenge the previous rigidity of party control. This is not necessarily a step in the direction of democratization, since a widening of rule to include the technical elite and sections of the intelligentsia may well represent a new version of elitism.

Meanwhile, in the capitalist societies, the same processes have resulted in a narrowing of actual democratic practice (at least in its parliamentary form), in the concentration of power in the hands of bureaucrats who seem to resemble their state socialist counterparts. Here, the analogy breaks down. In the state socialist regimes, concentrated (state) property was utilized by a political elite in the party to dominate and exploit society through the state. In the capitalist societies, concentrated property in its classical form was used as a direct means of exploitation: the propertied occupied and utilized the state insofar as necessary to maintain and extend economic domination. A certain modification of economic domination in the capitalist societies has been effected by political technicians extending state control, in the interests of the polity as a whole, to the market. By contrast, a certain loosening of extreme state domination in the state socialist regimes is taking place precisely through the progressive detachment of concentrated property from direct political control. The state socialist technicians, with their insistence on the relative autonomy of the economy and administration, have (to some considerable extent unwittingly) fragmented party power. In both cases, the technicians may occasionally legitimate themselves by referring to the higher public interests they ostensibly serve; in fact we may be witnessing a transfer of power rather than its subjugation to popular will.

A certain paradox attaches to one aspect of the analysis. I have insisted on the exceeding imperfection of pluralist institutions in the capitalist societies, on the ways in which

concentrated property can nullify (by distorting) democratic process. I have also suggested that the absence of
political pluralism accounts for the continuation of repression and authoritarianism in the state socialist regimes. Is
there any reason to think that pluralism can be institutionalized, more successfully, in the state socialist nations—
particularly since many of them lack democratic traditions?
In the end, a pluralism which pits the propertied against
the propertyless may prove less effective than one in which
all share in the control of property. There is a libertarian
current in socialism, now more prominent than it has been
for some time, which entails pluralist control of the administrative and productive process: producers' collectives,
workers' councils, autonomous agencies of cultural production, rotation of leadership in each. (In its contemporary western form, this current expresses itself in the still
highly schematic notions of "participatory democracy.")
For the moment, however, many of these reflections must
remain hypothetical: a pluralism of competing bureaucracies, legitimated periodically by popular electoral sanc-
tion, controlled by occasional legislative scrutiny and frequent criticism in the media of communication, is the most
we may now expect. Even this seems much: libertarian
critiques of power, in the capitalist and state socialist societies both, seem strongest amongst those (students, intellectuals, pure scientists) most remote from the administrative and productive process. The process effects its own
compliance. We may take some consolation from the suggestion implicit in recent events (the students' revolt, the
popular demand for political change in Czechoslovakia, the
protest of the American underclass, the restiveness of the
technical intelligentsia everywhere) that a perfect compliance with power is impossible. Inhumanly extended, it
can turn into its opposite.

CHAPTER THREE

CULTURE

THE PROBLEM of the distinctiveness of industrial culture confronts us at a moment when our conception of culture is undergoing drastic historical revision. The current question is not what new forms industrial society imposes upon culture but whether our present culture has retained sufficient elements of continuity with the past—even the recent past—to allow us to assume a continuity of human purpose through the convulsive changes which have succeeded one another since the industrial revolution. In a celebrated remark, André Malraux once declared that in the nineteenth century men asked if God was dead; today, we ask if man is dead. The responses often polarize about two positions. In the name of a previous conception of human purpose, as objectified in human symbolism and consciousness—or culture—many lament the decease of a secularized humanism directly descended from our religious legacy. Others insist that the willing acceptance of the obsolescence of old notions of man's capacities and works is the precondition for the development and enjoyment of new possibilities inherent in industrial society, just now become visible. The import of both responses is that only an historical perspective will enable us to understand the present crisis. I propose, after a brief introduction, to sketch the transition between bourgeois culture and early industrial culture, to depict, in other words, the industrialization of culture; to examine the contemporary problems of cultural stratification; and to consider some structural aspects of industrial culture from a critical but (I trust) not an impossibly ahistorical point of view.

I

The traditional Western definition of culture has been a unified one, developed before current distinctions between high culture and mass culture had any relevance. There were distinctions, profound distinctions, between high culture (accessible to the elite) and popular culture (accessible to all). These distinctions were important, of course, but equally important was the fact that both high culture and popular culture were continuous with a national past, that both shared common elements (originally religious), and that this community of culture made possible a good deal of communication between those who lived in different strata of the nation. Indeed, the social divisions of the European nations were often enough interpreted as cultural divisions, not least in Christian social theory: the exercise of power and the exercise of higher technique or thought were each legitimated as contributions to a common enterprise. The formal and conscious transmission of high culture across the generations, then, was not opposed to the relatively spontaneous transmission of popular culture. A concrete historical content united them both.

For present purposes, I shall designate that content as a conception, actualized in historical practice, of *Homo faber*. Man made his environment, altering the landscape through agriculture and agricultural technology, constructing towns and cities, concretizing his religious conceptions in cathedrals and in a variety of works of art, meeting his needs for work and play by devising a rhythmical calendar of days and months. The social constructions in which he lived, even if resting on domination, fraud, and exploitation, were on a human scale: If authority was sacralized, it was also concretized. Briefly, western culture throughout much of its historical trajectory was visibly man-made, the element of human intervention in and struggle against nature never entirely invisible, the very fragility of the distinction between culture and nature serving to emphasize the humanly generated quality of culture. These aspects of culture were continuous from the medieval period through the nineteenth century.

The development of a specific type of human mastery over nature, through the capacity for abstraction and scientific thought, had as a social precondition a certain division of cultural or intellectual labor. Science as a mode of mastery over nature has theological roots, in a system of belief which expressed a view of the world common to the bearers of high and popular culture. The development of scientific thought proper combined with artisanal and technological traditions (already very advanced by all historical standards) in late medieval Europe to bring on a new period of mastery over nature, with profound implications for the rest of culture. Brecht's *Galileo*, with its emphasis on the anticipation of the "new time," may in this respect be thought of as a more secular version of the Faust myth. With the introduction of science, high culture itself began to be divided: a division of intellectual labor set in, far more divisive in its implications than the previous division between priest and layman. The full development of this division waited upon the late nineteenth century, and it is worth noting that the eighteenth and early nineteenth centuries saw determined and relatively successful efforts to retain the unity of natural and human science. The Encyclopedia itself was amongst other things a compendium of technological innovation and scientific knowledge, as well as a program for the reconstruction of society and morals. Comte's attempted synthesis of social and scientific knowledge spoke for itself. Mill, and in their own way Engles and Marx, incorporated the natural sciences in their work.

The chief social characteristic of the division of intellectual labor up to the end of the nineteenth century was that it presupposed an intact high culture. That is to say (as the very violence of the Darwinian controversy proved) it presupposed an educated public to whom the results of scientific thought could be communicated. This assumption was largely correct. Its correctness, however, had other presuppositions. These were to be found less in the structure of culture itself than in the mode of culture's integration with the society. Until the late nineteenth century, European society was dominated by an elite which was an amalgam of bourgeois and aristocratic elements; it would be too crude to insist that the bourgeoisie was in the economy, particularly the urban and industrial economy, and the aristocracy in the state service and on the land. Rather, a backward glance will show that the aristocracy itself was a product of a continuous fusion between older aristocratic elements and a bourgeoisie which gradually assumed state and social functions hitherto reserved to the aristocracy (as with the French *noblesse de la robe*). For our purposes, we may state that the European elite was confident in the utilization of culture for its own social ends, a culture which it could apprehend, which had a definite boundary, which presented in principle no problems of opaqueness or inaccessibility. It was experienced as a means of mastery over the natural and historical environment rather than as a system which could or did escape understanding and control. The ordinary education in high culture offered to the European bourgeoisie was classical, in the sense that a large component of attention to Greek and Roman letters and thought was one of its fundaments. A certain conception of the utilization of culture, however, rendered natural science (also taught in the secondary schools which prepared the bourgeoisie for later education or for immediate entry into the occupational system) not alien to this tradition. This was in fact a later, more powerful, and for a time more confident and serene doctrine of *Homo faber*, attached to a social practice which seemed to verify the optimism of the nineteenth century. The generations of scientists, engineers and scientifically influenced philosophers in bourgeois Europe in this period were of course in conflict with certain resistances (often of a religious or ecclesiastical kind, sometimes in the form of a despairing skepticism—of the sort manifested by Kierkegaard or Dostoyevsky). They were nonetheless certain that both present and future belonged to them, and they expressed this confidence not in the conviction that they had displaced the older bourgeoisie in a cultural sense but that they were legitimate members of it.

The social and political convulsions of the turn of the century, which culminated in the First World War, did much to destroy this conviction. Behind these convulsions a long-term tendency was altering the structure of culture itself. As science and applied science occupied ever new areas of culture and society, the scientific enterprise lost its internal coherence. The precondition for the mastery of one discipline, or subdiscipline, became a renunciation of universality, not (as hitherto) its incorporation or expression in specialized scientific activity. The intellectual division of labor corresponded to the division of labor elsewhere in the productive system; it progressed and is progressing indefinitely, with no end in sight. As specialization became the characteristic of legitimate intellectual activity, an implicit renunciation of the claim that the whole of culture and society could be rationally apprehended emerged as a logical and psychological consequence. This process in culture, precisely as with the previous integration of culture and society, had structural bases in the movement of society itself.

At this distance in time from the nineteenth century, we are able to see that the epoch of a self-sufficient bourgeois culture was bound to end. The accumulation of productive forces, the necessity to co-ordinate an increasingly complex social and economic fabric, the sheer administrative imperatives implicit in the vast quantitative increase of European populations, rendered the self-sufficient bourgeois individual obsolete. It is quite true, of course, that by the beginning of industrialization the social division of labor had attained dimensions never reached historically. The division, however, at first functioned between large groups of persons, or social classes; the emergence of a new industrial bourgeoisie seemed to leave those in this category personally free to enjoy the advantages of their dominant class position. The notion of an individual career within this framework was attached to ideas of choice connected with the institution of the market. The bourgeois individual shaped himself by mastering an environment, in other words, already dominated by his class: the task of mastery was correspondingly easy, and some sort of harmony with the requisites of culture and with the mastery of the totality of the available high culture far easier to establish. But the market itself developed into a far more organized and differentiated structure within which the individual could not so easily move; concentrations of impersonal property became more important than individual property accumulation, and the very notion of a career altered. In brief, the epoch of bureaucratization was at hand. Mastery of culture no longer entailed an individual performance, of a virtuoso kind at its limits, but incorporation in a highly sequential and defined career sequence. Those in possession of a part of higher culture were necessarily aware that this was only a part, that it could be used only to make a part of an increasingly opaque whole function. The mastery of nature and society, once the mark of a self-confident bourgeoisie, was transmuted into the instrumentalization of knowledge as the bourgeoisie disappeared, to be replaced gradually by the forerunners of our own technical intelligentsia and technocratic elites.

Many see in these social groups the legitimate heirs of the high culture of the past. Literary intellectuals with their metaphysical scruples may agonize about history, it is argued, but the new dominant elements amongst the educated (those who master science and its applications) actually make history. Culture, on this argument, must express power or confess its irrelevance: the example of the Chinese Mandarinate at the end of Imperial China's history is the usual one, despite the fact that some who began in the Mandarinate ended as leaders of the Chinese Revolution. The suggestion that culture validates itself in a relationship to power is plausible enough, but at any given historical moment culture may contain possibilities unrealized or indeed impeded by the prevailing system of domination. Indeed, culture may have as one of its essential meanings a continual struggle against domination, temporarily abated in privileged periods, but invariably resumed as human purposes old and new fail to find objectification in society. The current wave of disturbances in industrial society deeply involves those called upon to perpetuate the present relationships between culture and power, the students apparently being prepared for posts in the technical intelligentsia and the technocratic elite. Our diagnosis of the significance of this revolt for the future of culture, in particular of high culture, must wait upon our analysis of its antecedents; here, let it be said, we cannot go back too far. Many of the younger radicals, especially in America, seem to lack an historical sense (although some of their leaders and spokesmen are admirable historians): an older radical can hardly dispense with one.

II

Industrial culture rests on the industrialization of culture. A system of symbols, of consciousness, of sensibility, of preconscious and unconscious meanings, has been assimilated to the imperatives of machine production, market organization, and bureaucratic power. That this has entailed deep alterations in the structure of culture itself is obvious; the culture subjected to these changes at the beginning of the nineteenth century was itself an historical precipitate, the result of the inner movement of bourgeois society. I have termed bourgeois culture a culture organized about the notion of *Homo faber:* the very term bespeaks an artisanal conception of activity, a visible, limited, and direct relationship to nature. From the late medieval period until the eighteenth century, high culture and popular culture were consonant: an artisanal idea of process may well have constituted one of their common elements. The artisan with his tools, the merchant with his account books, the state servitor with his legal codes, the early scientist with his rudimentary experimental apparatus, the philosopher with his reflections—each worked upon the matter before him in unmediated fashion. The division of social labor was quite advanced, and phenomena of exploitation and domination were exceedingly pronounced. The relatively small size of the populations organized by these activities, the apparent similarity of technique unifying the most diverse spheres of society, lent a certain unity to culture despite the division of labor and the concentration of power. Indeed, these last were legitimated often enough by imagery (almost invariably theological) which depicted society itself as an artifice, order as imposed upon a brute nature into which men could relapse if they failed to accept their stations.

Bourgeois culture, then, rested upon the domination of a limited market by a privileged class. That class, however, had to struggle for its privileges: against the threat of insubordination, sabotage, and revolt from below; against an aristocracy desperately unwilling to be ejected from power; against its own tendencies to inner dissolution. The unifying conception of *Homo faber* had a definite continuity over the centuries but it was constantly reinterpreted until with the industrial revolution it was (implicitly at first) situated in the market and the system of production itself. The change in the cultural conception of the locus of human power followed changes in the fundaments of religion and religiosity; these were generated in the struggle for a culture consonant with the changes in the position of the bourgeoisie in European society.

In its struggle for power, the bourgeoisie found the doctrine and practice of Protestantism especially congenial. The sanctification of work in the profane world, which endowed ordinary economic routine with a religious value; the doctrine of the priesthood of all believers, which undermined the immobility of a medieval society based primarily on hierarchy; the Calvinist disdain for the worship of the flesh, which had antitraditional consequences in politics; above all, perhaps, the depiction of the world (again in Calvinist doctrine and its psychological concomitants) as a field for unceasing, disciplined, and innovative labor *ad maiorem gloriam deum*—these were woven into the fabric of bourgeois culture. There were, of course, important national differences: the Lutheran doctrines accepted by German *Bürghertum* were far more compatible with a traditionalist and estate-organized society, and the great modern students of Protestantism's social consequences, Troeltsch and Weber, were themselves Germans who often deplored their own countrymen's political submissiveness. Troeltsch and Weber were modern students of the phenomenon, but it had been noted (in terms remarkably similar to those used by Weber in his classical essay *The Protestant Ethic and the Spirit of Capitalism*) by Comte and Marx. Weber (in a point sometimes overlooked by his epigones) also stressed the social and religious roots of early Protestantism in the way of life and religiosity of the late medieval cities, where the notion of a correspondence between work and its reward, of mastery over matter, were tangible components of the existence of the artisans and merchants who were the first bourgeoisie.

Protestantism in its Calvinist version was especially influential in Britain, the Netherlands, Scotland, and of course the New England colonies. Germany, with a bourgeoisie never able to challenge the aristocracy and therefore consigned indefinitely to the role of a state bourgeoisie, was Lutheran. France (where, to be sure, Calvinism was also espoused by a nobility seeking to take power from the Court) almost became a Protestant country; for centuries until the present day the social and cultural influence of the tiny Protestant group amongst the bourgeoisie has been immense. Moreover, French Catholicism was influenced by its Protestant rival. Jansenism, favored by the *noblesse de la robe,* or the state bourgeoisie, matched Protestantism in its spiritual rigor. At first glance, Italy seems to have been the society in which Protestantism made fewest inroads. Indeed, we may say that the unequivocally urban character of the Italian elite in the sixteenth and seventeenth centuries, the absence of a rural aristocracy of the type found north of the Alps, tempered their Catholicism and made Protestantism superfluous. Additionally, of course, the Church was Italian and the element of national protest in Protestantism was missing. The evidence, however, suggests that Calvinism was influential in cities like seventeenth-century Venice. Moreover, Savonarola was, in his ascetic rigor and demand for social and spiritual renewal, a Protestant in all but name—if a century ahead of the northern European Anabaptists whom he so strongly anticipated.

In a secular epoch, we sometimes overlook the ways in which our ancestors' entire culture, their interpretation of their social experience, was expressed in religious terms. Protestantism, in its variations, corresponded to the experience of the early modern bourgeoisie and constituted a set of beliefs, a ritual practice, an organization, which consolidated and validated their position in the world. More, it enabled them to impose their own culture— mediated by the new religion—upon other groupings, or alternatively to place these upon the defensive. Protestantism expressed and codified the position of the bourgeoisie in the social hierarchy, not in the narrow sense of a direct defense of their economic interests, but in the broader one of a symbolic integration of the many elements in bourgeois life. Eventually, of course, Protestantism (like any religious or cultural system) enjoyed a certain autonomy:

it shaped bourgeois experience as well as reflecting it. Even those versions of Protestantism which were antibourgeois, the chiliastic or quietistic Anabaptism derived from medieval heresies and biblical literalism, were slowly absorbed into bourgeois culture. The historians remember that the New England colonies were founded by men whose spiritual brethren in England were revolutionary; in our country's traditional self-interpretation, the colonists were models of civic rectitude.

It is certainly true that the fratricidal struggles of European Christendom in the Reformation and Counter Reformation eroded all ecclesiastical authority. Reformation doctrine, including the idea of the priesthood of all believers, was in the end contained in churches as repressive as the Catholic system against which the early reformers had revolted. Protestant doctrine, however, was a constant incitement to criticism of the reformed churches. In the seventeenth century in particular it constituted a critical force which pervaded all the spheres of culture. The Counter Reformation, meanwhile, was far from inducing ideological torpor in the Catholic countries. French Jansenism prepared the way for that bourgeois skepticism which was later to facilitate the Enlightenment. The inner movement of European religious belief, particularly in its effects on a literate bourgeoisie, contributed to the latter's spiritual self-emancipation.

Systematic inquiry into the natural world, the development of canons of scientific procedure, and the institutionalization of scientific discourse in intellectual life were of course amongst the decisive sources of secularization. Modern science itself had religious roots. The Calvinist notion of the autonomy of the world has been depicted by Weber as a source of the process termed rationalization. This entailed the increasing penetration of all spheres of

culture by criteria of rational calculation and predictability. The cultural precondition for our bureaucratized
social organization, rationalization had amongst its fundaments the related conceptions of the propriety and possibility of scientific investigation and technological innovation. These were encouraged by the peculiarities of the
Calvinist interpretation of the autonomy of the world:
God in his dreadful majesty was remote from a world
which was therefore susceptible to examination and alteration. There were also Catholic sources for the secular conception of the autonomy of the world. Medieval Catholicism itself, with its conception of a God immanent in nature and society, was not so impossibly discontinuous
with our experience as a crude historiography would have
us believe. The spiritual origins of modern science are to
be found as much in scholasticism and medieval pantheism
as in Calvinism. Every theological system has a doctrine
which can be transmuted into a doctrine of the autonomy
of the world. Transmutation actually occurs when the real
order of society becomes restive about the total control of
culture by the Church.

III

These were some of the elements in early bourgeois culture which were later transmuted into industrial culture.
Before we can understand that transformation, we have to
examine the institutions of early bourgeois culture. That
culture was urban; its centers of development and diffusion were in the cities, and from these it radiated outward.
It was urban, however, in a special sense. The shift of economic and political power to the cities meant that urban
markets dominated the processes of exchange, that the
absolutistic state's court and administration were concen-

trated in national and provincial capitals. The new urban high culture incorporated the new dimensions of social experience in its symbolic language. The processes of production and exchange in national and international markets, the new social and political importance of those in command of these processes, expressed themselves in a new set of social conventions and a new metaphysic. As the bourgeoisie contended with the aristocrats for command of the absolutistic state, the conflict engendered a new life style and a new world picture in which the specifically bourgeois modes of mastery over nature and society were represented. The urban component in early bourgeois high culture, then, was a consequence of that culture's constitution about urban processes and ideas. This explains the apparent paradox of the English Calvinist gentry, cultivating advanced scientific and theological ideas in their country houses; of the inability of the French aristocracy to resist the intellectual subversion cultivated in Parisian and provincial *salons;* of the urban *habitus* of the elites in the Italian city states.

Domination in agrarian society was direct and brutal; domination and exploitation in urban society was mediated. Urban intellectuality in part was a response to this characteristic of urban life: social processes seemingly remote or autonomous had to be explained. At the same time, the relatively passive participation of the agrarian populace in politics had no urban equivalent: forms of popular representation developed early in medieval Europe. If economic processes were frequently opaque in the cities, they collided with traditions of community which insisted upon visibility and public accountability in all of social life. The cities were loci of nascent capitalist enterprise and showplaces of unrestrained avarice; their populations at the same time strove to maintain their institutional capacities to resist these forces. In the resultant conflicts, bourgeois justifications of wealth had to contend with traditions of popular criticism. The cities were of course centers for the circulation of goods and persons. The intensity of their internal conflicts combined with these other crossroads functions to render them especially receptive to new ideas. From the medieval period onward, heresy and orthodoxy, conservatism and innovation, contended in the cities. Precisely because the bourgeoisie insisted on developing and promulgating their own version of high culture, that culture was open to emendation, not infrequently radical emendation, from within: its elaboration and diffusion were entrusted to specialists who often had eccentric positions with respect to the main elements of bourgeois routine.

The diffusion of culture within and beyond the cities was revolutionized by the invention of printing toward the end of the fifteenth century. (The university lecture, as a means of intellectual communication, had its origins in a period when books were in manuscript. That it has remained an essential element of academic technology since is not unequivocal evidence for the innovative capacities of the universities.) The course of the Protestant Reformation is unthinkable without printing, even if but 5 or 10 per cent of Luther's contemporaries were literate. These were concentrated in the urban population, and where (as amongst some artisans and many peasants) readers were few in certain groups, those with literacy communicated the new ideas orally to the others. Printing greatly enlarged the public scope of culture by making possible a rapid and wide diffusion of matters previously arcane. It was the technical precondition for a new system of cultural stratification, more complex and differentiated than the medieval one, and with more opportunity for the expression not only of difference but of dissensus. Finally, it occasioned profound changes in the structure of intellectual institutions, not least by expanding the demand for intellectuals.

The first new intellectual occupation was that of the printers. Their own role in the Reformation could be termed legendary, were the legends not rooted in historical fact: the printers of Zurich and of Lyons were important agents of religious agitation. The printers through the subsequent centuries were to retain a certain critical independence: artisans who worked with their hands, yet often educated to a bourgeois level, in the nineteenth century many were amongst the first working-class socialists. The master artisans in possession of printing presses were the first publishers; Frobenius of Basel competed with contemporary merchants and princes to subsidize Erasmus. With the development of publishing as an enterprise, new economic forms of intellectual activity became possible: thinkers were no longer exclusively dependent upon patronage or some institutional affiliation, but could exist (if rarely in practice until the eighteenth century) from royalties. Direct support of intellectual production by a public purchasing intellectual products on a free market came relatively late, in the eighteenth century in England and afterward elsewhere. We shall see that the notion of an intellectual free market, which once promised liberation from the rigidified cultural traditions guarded by particular interests, in industrialism eventually led to oligopolistic and monopolistic domination of public intellectual life. For the moment, let us consider the beginnings of the new public culture.

Printing entailed the possibility of breaching the barriers of family, community, and estate to unify far larger segments of society (and eventually, all of it) in a literate public. Equipped with the cultural resources which often engendered criticism of tradition and convention (and, behind these, of the concrete interests they legitimated and maintained), a literate public was a potential threat to the social order. Yet wider literacy was also a condition of the exercise of new types of social discipline, a means of diffusing models of belief and comportment. Direct ecclesiastical and political censorship of the written word was practically universal in Europe up to the French Revolution (England excepted). The essential control functions were implicitly delegated, however, to the institutions of intellectual life, chartered to define and organize culture in a manner consonant with the requirements, psychological and political, of the existing bourgeois order.

In Protestant Europe, the Reformation had destroyed the omnipresent authority of the Roman Church, to substitute for it a new set of ecclesiastical institutions. A radical improvement in the educational and moral qualifications of the new clergy, the organization of a total educational system, and the promulgation of a Protestant culture in precept and word made of these institutions far more effective agencies of cultural direction than the decomposing late medieval Church. Lay governance in early Protestantism meant close community supervision of daily routine, in urban circumstances in which an escape into privacy was impossible. In due course, the Protestant personality emerged to internalize the precepts of Protestant conduct, but in fact that personality was the individuated expression of a situation in which community, class, and family were spiritually organized by a Church integrated with each. We celebrate Protestantism as an important source of the principle of free examination in European culture and in retrospect, we overlook the extent to which successive Protestant heterodoxies had to revalidate the principle in renewed struggles against Protestant authority.

A particular Protestant attitude to work and social duty was engendered by this extremely effective system for the diffusion and implantation of a culture. It was a system in which the inclinations of the public were reinforced by the import of the cultural demands made upon it: the profane derivatives of Protestant belief corresponded to imperatives which were inextricable elements of bourgeois life. In Protestantism, moreover, a process of cultural production and one of consumption were not counterposed. The clergy and religious and moral tractarians proposed; the laity disposed, and each lay life was (in theory at least) a work of self-reflection. The novel, the great bourgeois art form, was in its beginnings a Protestant experience, an account of a moral career.

The culture of the Counter Reformation reflected an entirely different system of political domination and moral tutelage. Counter-Reformation intellectuality was more severely limited to clerics. The laity were educated and informed according to stratified categories of power and sensibility, the Church guarding for itself the right to control access to culture. Where as in Jansenist France the urban bourgeoisie resembled its Protestant confreres elsewhere, a variant of Catholic religiosity emerged which was not unlike Protestantism. Alternatively, as in eighteenth-century France, an anticlerical and antireligious sentiment became the cultural focus of bourgeois striving for political and social domination. In other Counter-Reformation societies an educated bourgeoisie tolerated a contemptuous tutelage of the masses, in the interest of maintaining its own position in the social hierarchy. Here, the bourgeoisie was usually unwilling or unable to challenge the aristocracy on its own. This was the case in Germany (even in Lutheran Germany to some considerable extent) and above all in southern Europe. The aesthetic and sensual emphases of Counter-Reformation culture, the restriction of its intellectuality to privileged elites and carefully controlled centers of activity, gave to Catholic European culture a political cast which only the French Revolution was to shake. Paradoxically, its reactionary aspect when contrasted with Protestant bourgeois culture expressed a fundamental human engagement which in the end may enable Catholicism to adapt to industrialism. The stratification of the community in cultural terms was justified by a preindustrial idea of the sacredness of community which enabled Catholicism, at certain times and certain places, to resist the implacable demands of the market. That Catholic thinkers and trade unions are today in the vanguard of the European left (as the outbreak in France in the spring of 1968 has shown) is due to an idea of community which can imply not only the necessity of protecting that community by cultural tutelage but also of fulfilling it by radically expanding participation in it.

Both Reformation and Counter Reformation gave new life and new shape to the European universities. An educated clergy was required by both churches, and doctrine had to be defended and reshaped. Concurrently, the absolutistic state's need for legists, the bourgeois economy's demand for lawyers, placed new demands upon the faculties of law. The general increase in intellectual activity attendant upon continuing urbanization and the increasing domination of the bourgeoisie was only imperfectly contained, however, within the universities, which did not assume their modern tasks until the nineteenth century. Patronage, the learned societies, independent journals, and independent production for the intellectual market were among the forms of cultural activity which flourished in bourgeois society.

Patronage, the direct subsidization of cultural production by states, courts of persons, was of course an optimal mode of ensuring that the final product was acceptable to the patron. Erasmus, who made desperate efforts to maintain himself between the fronts during the outbreak of Europe's religious wars in the sixteenth century, was perhaps a classical example of the difficulties of intellectual subsistence under conditions of patronage. The form, at any rate, seemed more effective with respect to creation in the plastic arts and music than to spheres of high culture with more direct metaphysical and social content. I have said that the allocation of intellectual production to specialists entailed a margin of freedom from direct control of production by those immersed in ordinary bourgeois routine. It is significant, in this connection, that some of the most original spirits of the early bourgeois epoch were between two historical worlds: lesser nobles at the frontiers of cultural creation and relatively immune to immediate pressures. The most favorable circumstances for a culture relatively free of direct constraints—whatever the indirect ones in effect—entail groupings or associations (however loose in organizational form) of intellectuals.

These conditions were met, in the early bourgeois epoch, in several ways. The learned societies grouped men pursuing particular intellectual interests, often collected and redistributed funds, and were particularly effective in encouraging the early development of the natural sciences—by providing a setting congenial to innovations refused by the universities and the churches. Other sets of intellectuals gathered in private *salons* or in the quasi-public setting of coffee houses and cafés. Still others were grouped in joint editorial ventures, in reviews or more ambitious projects still, of which the French *Encyclopédie* was the supreme example. With an initial subscription list of

4,500, this compendium appealed to the public not only because of its summary of existing knowledge but on account of its moral and political program—nothing less than the reconstitution of society on the basis of enlightenment. The very project presupposed the existence of a public receptive to its message, but much of the message still had to be phrased in elliptical, ironic, or euphemistic terms.

Publics, as distinct from patrons, could enable intellectuals to work in relatively independent fashion only when the views of the intellectuals were consonant with public receptivity. In these circumstances, publics could effectively nullify censorship or circumvent the transmission of culture by official instances. In seventeenth-century England, an entire network of Puritan cultural activity developed in opposition to the Church of England. In eighteenth-century France, the venerable Sorbonne was increasingly the butt of contempt, the Church itself undermined by deistic clerics who found the *Encyclopédie* more to their taste than scholastic theology. Meanwhile, servitors of the *ancien régime* crowded the Parisian *salons* whose literary lions were single-mindedly devoted to the regime's extirpation. These, however, were occasions upon which the older forms of bourgeois culture were no longer compatible with the exigencies of bourgeois life, when the state in particular mobilized its repressive forces in the service of a culture unacceptable to the class striving for domination in society. When the officially promulgated culture and the aspirations and actual life of the bourgeoisie were in rough concordance, the more critical intellectuals found themselves more isolated, their ideas seemed impossibly remote from reality, even if, later, these ideas were to become common property of the children of those

who had earlier received them with hostility or incom-
prehension.

The Enlightenment in France was both the last univer-
sally significant outbreak of preindustrial culture and an
anticipation of the new society. France, constricted by the
ancien régime, had barely begun the process of industrialization—but critical spirits in France looked across the
Channel at England, already richer on account of machine
production, socially and politically freer. The intellectuals
of the Enlightenment elaborated the demands of the
French bourgeoisie into a program for a new humanity, a
program which proved impossible of realization in the
industrial epoch precisely because of the domination of
a bourgeoisie in possession and control of the machines
which could have liberated humanity from many of its
ancient burdens.

The Enlightenment demanded the end of the conventional and legal divisions in society which divided it into
estates. The estates disappeared, but the equality which
replaced it was a formal equality in a market system which
continually reproduced its own inequalities of property
and power. The Enlightenment promulgated a new human
morality, but the morality which emerged, free of theological tutelage, was subject to the implacable control of a
class which exercised tutelage over all others as well as itself. The Enlightenment held that the establishment of
nature's laws by science could be followed by a true moral
science, a description of the ways in which men could fulfill their own nature by living in intelligence and harmony.
Intelligence and harmony in the conduct of human affairs
have since not been conspicuous, and the debate over
human nature has continued angry and unresolved. The
bourgeoisie did advance into a new culture, but that cul-

ture quickly escaped its own control and assumed terrifyingly autonomous dimensions. We now confront the industrialization of culture itself.

IV

The industrialization of culture entailed the gradual extirpation of *Homo faber*. The notion of man acting upon nature and society persisted. In fact, mastery was expressed in techniques for the control of nature and mechanisms of social discipline which gradually assumed the appearance of autonomous forces. Culture, in other words, was increasingly objectified. That objectification reflected the objectification of human labor power in the processes of machine production, and the abstract expression of human social relationships in the impersonal forces of the market. To what extent objectification is due to machine production irrespective of the social organization of the productive process remains an open question: certainly, the experience of the state socialist societies affords no unequivocal answer. It is insufficient, however, to consider objectification without analyzing the concrete forms it has taken in its inexorable historical progression.

The industrialization of culture began with an act of destruction: the elimination of artisan and peasant culture as artisans and peasants were transformed into an industrial proletariat. This proceeded unequally in the several nations. Certainly, phenomena like the difference in quality between English and French cooking are related to the unequal impact of industrialization upon the rural populations in each country. The emergence of an industrial proletariat meant more than the subjection of large groups to totally new and often cruelly different and exacting work routines. It altered their relationships to nature

and to material, transformed their communities, tore up
the very tissue of their lives. Those directly subjugated to
the machine soon formed a huge enclave within society,
culturally far more remote from the rest of it than had
been their peasant and artisan ancestors.

I have just spoken of the subjugation of men (and
women) to the machine. In fact, they were subjugated by
other men, who owned the machines. As new forms of
domination developed, the older forms of bourgeois culture also gave way. A new and crude brutality replaced, for
a time at least, the formed self-cultivation of the bourgeois
individual. The first capitalist generations were, often
enough, primitive in the pejorative sense. They seemed to
incorporate in their own lives the rapacity, calculation,
and depersonalization of the market. This was especially
true, of course, of those who acceded to industrial property
without having been inducted into the culture which expressed previous modes of bourgeois existence. Again, the
nations which experienced either a late or partial industrialization retained more continuity with their cultural
past: France, Germany, Italy, and Russia may be contrasted in this respect with Britain and the United States.
In each of the continental societies, important elite groups
constituted themselves as bearers of values and beliefs
other than those of the market. They were far from renouncing power, but their manner of exercising it did not
involve them directly in the market. The domination of
the economy by machine production did impress itself
upon their culture; as time went on, their own traditions
were adapted to the exigencies of industrial existence. It
was, however, an adaptation which often assured to industrial society the very continuity of culture which its own
inner movement seemed to deny. Begun in the eighteenth
century, that movement is still not complete. We are in our

own generation witnesses, however, to one of its climaxes; even the continuities assured by the survival of certain pre-industrial traditions are now in doubt.

Aesthetic sensibility, religious feeling (above all, the belief in transcendence), the emotions between persons, sensuality itself, were transformed by the new industrial setting. The artisans and peasants lost the forms which had regulated the rhythmical alternation of work and leisure; their communities, organized about that alternation, now became appendages of the factories. The most highly cultured of the bourgeoisie were excluded from the new processes of production. They sensed that their former world, with its consonance between work and culture, was gone. In the sphere of politics, the conflicts engendered by the French Revolution accentuated this conviction: intended to construct a new community, it ended both with some of the ancient powers restored and with some repellent new ones in command. A turn to inwardness, to feeling and imagination, and often enough to an idealized past or mythic future, was a consequence for the more sensitive, particularly for those who specialized in the transmission of culture, the intellectuals and artists. The Romantic movement had many aspects, but in one of them it expressed this remoteness from the market and the machine.

What of the others, those not entirely agonized by the historical transition and closer to the structures of administration, exchange, and production: the civil servants, merchants, and the emergent professionals? For these, the maintenance of order was now equivalent to the maintenance of industrial property. Not themselves proprietors of the new means of production, they conceived of its defense as in their own interest, since they equated their ability to pursue individualized careers to the "liberty" attached to limitless rights over property. The modern notion and substance of a career, a precipitate of the enlarged scale and increased mobility of industrial society, had important psychological consequences. It led to a certain instrumentalization of culture, a constriction of personal perspective to the private sphere, a disassociation of ethics from a conception of community. Its most immediate correlate was in the externalization of religion, the ascription to the churches of the functions of social control and a severe diminution in their effective spiritual authority. A separation of private feeling from public life led to the impoverishment of both, an impoverishment not fundamentally relieved by the continuation of religious forms emptied of their traditional content, the idea of transcendence.

Meanwhile, the indispensable role of technology in the production process led to the formation and gradual enlargement of a technically educated and employed group within the bourgeoisie. The cultural implications were two. Firstly, this was a continuation of the relentless progression of science and a scientific world view—which had so many destructive consequences for traditional cultural syntheses, particularly in the sphere of religion. Some, like the Saint-Simonians (and in more subtle ways, the utilitarians in England), supposed that all of society could be reorganized on scientific principles, and directed in effect by social technologists. This "scientistic" program constituted an industrial utopia, but in fact its realization has proven impossible. The comportment of the technologists suggested a remarkable compartmentalization in their personal culture. They were (and are) quite capable of applying technology in the production process, while accepting the multiple irrationalities of the larger society and its culture. Indeed, the institutionalization of science and technology heightened those irrationalities, by releasing forces which few could comprehend and almost none control. This led in turn to the split between science and humanistic culture, much discussed recently but actually first visible in the nineteenth century. The recent debate has been curiously arid, since much of it has depicted the scientists as the actual and legitimate heirs of *Homo faber,* and the humanists as pathologically nostalgic for an outmoded version of culture. *Homo faber,* however, has been fragmented. The active component of culture, altering nature and society, has been allocated to science and technology. The meaningful one, the human self-interpretation which alone could make sense of this activity has been ascribed to those devoid of any practical competence. No resolution of this dilemma is in sight.

V

The industrialization of culture imposed upon cultural activity models of comportment, standards of judgment, and forms of organization derived from the processes of machine production themselves. The very notion of a mass culture presupposes a material capacity, on the part of those in command of the cultural market, to treat large publics as composed of cultural consumers—themselves incapable of organization in their own interests. The improvement of techniques in printing, the subsequent invention of radio and television, constitute but one element in this situation of cultural domination. The fact of domination itself has been at least as important, domination exercised through possession or command of the means of cultural production.

The division of labor has also marked industrial culture. The increasing complexity of culture, its impenetrability as a whole, the length of time required for mastery of any of its segments, the imposition upon culture of standards of efficiency or profitability derived directly from the market, have resulted in a fragmentation of the cultural labor force. The phenomenon is far more subtle and pervasive than a mere distinction between producers, distributors, and consumers. It is less a question of circuits of exchange for finished cultural products than of alterations in the nature of the product. Culture no longer concretizes itself in individual relationships to nature and society, but in an enormous multiplicity of forms, processes, and entities which seem independent, detached from their origin in human activity. The significance of the very notion of a cultural product may now be somewhat more clear. It is a mode of discourse which accepts the fact of what I earlier termed the objectification of culture, a gap (indeed, an abyss) between men and the meanings and mechanisms of a world they are not quite able to experience as theirs. The idea of a cultural product appears to have emerged precisely when men became incapable of engendering a new culture. The residual meaningfulness of the work of individuals was lost in the senselessness of the whole. A lack of meaning in work for many, at the same time, was transposed into meaning for society at a distance very remote from their lives.

The cultural division of labor has proceeded in two ways. Horizontal distinctions separate those with equal access to culture. These are often enough distinctions of function: literary and plastic artists, engineers and scientists, lawyers and philosophers, shape symbols and materials which are used with different degrees of comprehension by their publics. Here, important differences of power and influence intrude. Some work for publics, who are free to accept or reject particular instances of culture which are more or less autonomously conceived and produced. Others, now in the majority, work for employers who dictate conception and production alike. Meanwhile, vertical distinctions of an extreme kind constitute a cultural stratification of the population. Differences in wealth, income, and occupation are most commonly expressed through differences in education. Increasingly, educational institutions have replaced the churches as sites for the organization and transmission of culture. The social stratification of systems of education, their almost mechanical alignment with class systems, is striking.

Let us consider, briefly, the case of the universities. The modern university system has many roots in the Europe of the Middle Ages, the Renaissance, and the Reformation. Its distinctively modern forms, however, date from the beginning of the nineteenth century. The French Revolution expelled the priests from the Sorbonne and proposed to place the universities at the service of reason. Napoleon gave this a precise content: the universities were to prepare a technical and political elite. In Prussia, von Humboldt sketched a design for the new university of Berlin. The cultivation of science and scholarship, he declared, was the most effective means to form character, to give men moral power over material circumstance. In fact, the German university prepared an academically educated class for specialized bureaucratic functions. The awakening of Oxford from its eighteenth-century somnolence followed, first in the middle of the nineteenth century and coinciding with the reform of the British higher civil service, its opening to the middle class. Reflection on classical philosophy, at Oxford, in the end shaped an imperial elite. The universities, in all three cases, were the privileged channels for access to important political functions. At the same time, they claimed a monopoly, in effect, of high cultural production and diffusion. In certain areas, particularly the scientific and technical ones, they were able to make good their monopolistic claims: they alone had the appropriate means of cultural production. What is most striking, however, about the universities in this period is the extent to which they induced class-specific attitudes to work and the world—inextricably fused with the specific forms and content of the high culture they transmitted. The universities, as secular agencies for the disciplining of the potentially disruptive forces of culture, have performed this function until the present. Their current crisis is connected with the obvious erosion of their claim to monopolize high culture, less because of the challenge of other agencies than because of the progressive decomposition of high culture itself. Their class-specific training functions, of course, have continued—into a situation in which their previously narrow class basis is a source of social disruption rather than a mode of social integration.

The universities have been at the apex of the system of cultural stratification. The interpenetration of academic and political elites reminds us of the political functions of this system: culture has served in industrial society as a vehicle of domination. Educational systems have been chartered to transmit just so much knowledge as was supposed (by their rulers) to be good for the social classes with access to them. The press and the mass media, popular publications (whether politically censored or not) have propagated images of the world which have reinforced its dreadful immanence. They have conveyed crude versions of consensual ideologies, they have denied by implication the possibilities of realizing alternative social arrangements which would reverse or seriously alter the prevailing distribution of power, and above all they have mounted a savage attack on those powers of imagination and sensibility which alone could mobilize psychic energies for criticism or revolt. In catering to sensuality (as in popular pornography), the culture imposed upon the mass of the population has reinforced existing systems of psychological and moral constraint. It has done so by providing compartmentalized and fictive outlets for impulses which might otherwise disrupt familial and other institutions. Mass culture in this respect is an instrument of discipline. The hopes of the nineteenth-century liberals that it might become a means of elevation and cultural liberation are piteously far from fulfilled.

I have written, above, of the restriction of perspective to the private sphere as a consequence of the industrialization of culture. Where the division of labor has extended to the renewal (or reproduction) of the symbolic substance of society, family, neighborhood, and workplace have lost their significance as foyers of culture. The radical break between familial routine, daily human contacts, work and higher culture, has made of this last something narrowly symbolic—devoid of an infusion of instinctual energy and lacking an emplacement in routine. The development in the family, neighborhood, and workplace of partial or limited systems of meaning, often without direct relationship to the larger structure of society or the movement of higher culture, has had terrible consequences. Precisely as higher culture has become infinitely more complex, most inhabitants of industrial society have become culturally more constricted or impoverished. The theoretic possibility of a qualitatively new human mastery of the environment remains. In practice, the higher culture which could liberate new human potentials is encapsulated in forms of organizations which effectively deny this possibility.

VI

National differences, often subsuming political ones, have varied the incidence of these general tendencies. In the United States, the absolute domination of free market capitalism has combined with the Puritan ethic to push high culture into a pronouncedly disfavored place. Activity has been valued, rather than thought, and inwardness (in contradistinction to a cheaply exteriorized sentimentality) distrusted. Public and private conscience have been split, and high culture has been the domain of self-constituted private groups, at first the churches and later class-specific patrons of one or anther sort. Manifestly, high culture did not pay, and this accounted in large part for the absence of public sponsorship of it. The parvenu status of a population composed increasingly of the descendants of those who had fled from Europe without partaking of its high culture reinforced these trends. The recent reversal in the public evaluation of culture is most apparent in certain spheres, as in the financing of higher education and scientific research, without central co-ordination of which no industrial society could survive. The philistinism so unashamedly proclaimed by those who once led what was euphemistically described as a "business civilization" has now given way to the endorsement of technical-scientific expertise. (The value and potency of this is, in America, grotesquely overestimated.) A humanistic culture is to be found, meanwhile, academicized in the universities or as an object of consumption amongst the leisured, but its relationship to the self-definition of the national community is extremely tenuous. The young, clearly, in America as elsewhere have different ideas.

These have as yet to take institutional form—if, indeed, they ever can.

In Britain, free market capitalism and Puritanism have had to contend with an aristocratic tradition, although the fusion of traditions has been facilitated by the readiness of the aristocracy to draw benefits from capitalism. Again, as in the United States, a public conception of culture has been wanting. In contrast with America, however, the private groupings interested in higher culture were practically identical with the national elites. These developed in the nineteenth and early twentieth centuries a peculiar version of high culture, and they were quite open as to its class character: culture, for them, was what the lower middle class and (even more) the workers lacked. Not surprisingly, these classes developed counter-cultures of their own. In no society have cultural and class divisions been so neatly matched. The encapsulation of the working class in its own mode of comportment has continued well into the epoch of the alleged destruction of these differences by mass culture or the development of national patterns of consumption. Part of the source of Britain's striking lack of adaptability to the conditions of modern administrative and industrial technology may reside in the persistence of these barriers, which make a common system of education more difficult to implant in Britain than elsewhere. Meanwhile, the educated continue to congratulate themselves on their "empiricism," without quite seeing that British "empiricism" was a highly conventional and unreflective way of doing things, in a stable political environment. The environment having become less stable, "empiricism" has continued as a rigidified caricature of its former self. The same may be said of certain other conventions. The more sensual aspects of the recent London scene assume, in this connection, a curiously com-

pulsive aspect: in a culture stuck in the early twentieth century, the assimilation of freedoms attained over two generations by others must come with a jerk.

On the continent, by contrast, culture and especially
higher culture has—despite the obvious class characteristics attached to it—been defined as a national or public
concern. The cultural apparatus in France (schools, universities, museums, and theaters) has often enough taken
on the mission of a republican counter-church, and has at
times acted as the conscience of the French revolutionary
tradition. In Germany, the same apparatus has manifested
an obsessional adherence to the existing state, a bureaucratic conformism. In both cases, however, a certain cultural cohesion has developed in the national community
as a result of the public character of its cultural institutions. France and Germany, additionally, have been less
remote from their preindustrial pasts. The peasantry, an
important part of the bourgeoisie in each society, a considerable aristocratic residuum different in kind from the
British type, artisanal traditions amongst the workers,
above all perhaps the pervasive influence of the churches
(despite anticlericalism in France and its less powerful
counterpart in Germany), have each contributed to a cultural continuity ruptured in Britain by the industrial revolution and missing in America.

It is true that in France the bourgeoisie has been
divided. One has only to read the astonishing memoirs of
Simone de Beauvoir to see the differences: on the one
hand, we find a narrow and indeed Puritanical Catholic
bourgeoisie, concerned with money, family, and order. On
the other we discover a bohemian and cosmopolitan set of
intellectuals, disdainful of ordinary routine, profoundly
critical of their society, and yet deeply attached to some of
its political traditions and their rhetorical expressions.

Between the two, perhaps, we may identify a group (embracing large numbers in the bourgeoisie) perfectly at home in routine and at the same time ideologically commited to a Jacobin interpretation of national community. "La coeur à gauche, le portefeuille à droit" (The heart on the left, the wallet on the right) would appear to characterize this group. The explicit politicization of high culture has gone very far in France: all parties to any cultural debate are likely to show awareness of the political implications of their views. What is striking is the way in which political debate between and amongst parties bitterly at odds on the future of the nation manifests common assumptions as to the function and content of high culture in the national community. The notion of the nation as in the last resort serving the maintenance and recreation of higher culture ("la mission civilisatrice"—France's civilizing mission) expresses a secularized interpretation of national community with religious roots. It is significant that the political demands of the organized working class invariably include demands for full participation in the national cultural patrimony. The (admittedly precarious) co-existence since the French Revolution of bourgeois routine and bohemian cultural innovation, of bourgeois domination and working-class challenge, of Catholicism and laicism, has proven so fruitful in the sphere of culture precisely because of a common language. The continuation into an industrial epoch of these conceptions, combined with the absurdly backward aspects of much of French social organization, in May of 1968 provoked a convulsion. Typically, French debate about the convulsion has been concerned to a considerable extent with restoring the fragmented unity of the cultural community.

French culture is indeed bourgeois culture, and its problem has been the assimilation of industrial experience.

German culture has never expressed the life style of a politically independent bourgeoisie, but has encompassed the enforced fusion in industrial circumstances of bureaucratic state servitors and early bourgeois spiritual traditions. The traditions were spiritual not only because of the religious peculiarities of Germany, especially its Lutheran heritage, but also because of the continuing powerlessness of the German bourgeoisie. The turn to a highly spiritualized inner life, the ostensible separation of culture from politics, reflected this group's inability to master its historical environment. The celebrated split in German consciousness, between extreme inwardness and spirituality, bureaucratic and legalistic pedantry, and technological efficiency, expresses the co-optation of the bourgeoisie by their society's agencies of power. The intellectuals could oppose to power only their belief in the redeeming sphere of the spirit—with the result that a politically powerless spirituality was quickly enough vulgarized into an ancillary of the state. The universities, which elsewhere harbored some critical reflection on state and society, in Germany concentrated on the provision of legists and technologists for state and industry. Humanistic and social studies, insofar as they touched upon political matters, were generally conservative. (Max Weber's defense of the possibility of objectivity in the social sciences was directed at his conservative colleagues.) An oppositional culture was attempted by the working-class movement, but it was curiously doctrinal in its emphases: the actual style of life of the German workers was too close to that of their lower-middle-class compatriots to generate cultural independence. The desperate political protests of the radical intellectuals, from Marx and Heine to Dutschke, often translated into German models of thought and politics originally French. The one relatively cosmopolitan and liberal group in German cultural life, an important fraction of the German Jewish intellectuals, had to pay a bitter price for their cosmopolitanism—which was resented not least by many of the educated Germans.

German public culture, then, has often been resolutely philistine. French public culture has been marked by its class character. The public nature of cultural institutions in the two societies, however, contains possibilities for radical transformations in the implantation of culture—once the balance of forces in the public sphere changes. The definition of culture as not simply a matter of private choice but as a matter of public concern precludes the total seizure of culture by the apparatus of industrial production and the mechanisms of the market. The preindustrial components in French and German culture, then, paradoxically entail the possibility of a transformation of cultural institutions in advanced industrial circumstances. The transformation has not taken place, although many are thinking about it. The Revolution of May, 1968, in Paris, the continuing disturbances in the German universities, are indications that the young (and some of their elders, at least) have in this respect proceeded from reflection to action. The demand that cultural institutions be governed democratically, that they serve the nation and not a class, the vision of a culture become both public and free of tutelage—these are no longer quite utopian but have become components of a political program.

The example, in this connection, of the state socialist societies is instructive. That the control of culture by the state parties in the several countries (above all in the Soviet Union) is invariably narrow and dogmatic and often cretinous; that scientists, writers and artists have mounted a continuing campaign against this form of authoritarianism; that the students in the state socialist societies are also participants in that generational conflict which is now sweeping across borders—these points hardly require iteration. The notion of control by the producers of the means of production, however, does lend weight to the demands of the intellectuals in these societies that they be freed of tutelage. The very complexity of the division of intellectual labor works in their favor, particularly in scientific fields. If and when the intellectuals do appropriate their own means of production, they will do so in a social and cultural atmosphere which (whatever the deformations of the libertarian ideals of socialism and whatever the defects caused by an absence of pluralistic cultural institutions) is free of the cheap commercialism found in our own societies. Domination by a ruling party (as the Yugoslav and Czech examples perhaps show) may be easier to overthrow in the sphere of culture than the pervasive domination and degradation resulting from the application of criteria of marketability to culture.

VII

I have, thus far, written rather abstractly about an entity termed high culture. I have done so in essays developed from talks to a university public, and which are likely to be read in the universities. In the circumstances, perhaps I can concretize the discussion somewhat by dealing with the crisis of the universities, which refracts the crisis of contemporary culture itself. I shall deal with the western European universities, which are closest perhaps to certain traditional conceptions of high culture. My readers will not find it difficult to extrapolate, if they wish, to the American situation.

The locus of high culture has shifted; indeed, there is no longer one setting for it. The culture-bearing elite has been fragmented into a political and bureaucratic elite with control of techniques of administration and applied science; an aesthetic and literary avant-garde with political attitudes which range from oppositional to withdrawn; a scholarly and scientific group in the universities with no particular connection with power, the uses of which it may approve of or disapprove of but to which it has no consistent or unequivocal relationship. That these somewhat sharp categories in fact overlap is clear; it is equally clear that these three groups no longer speak to a unified public and that no consensus exists as to what cultural activities are of value. The phenomenon of marketing, by which certain tendencies in avant-garde culture are transformed into popular or semipopular articles, is in fact evidence for the irrelevance of avant-garde effort: once intended to create new forms of experience against the resistance of the philistines, avant-garde activity is now a spectator sport for the philistines themselves. Meanwhile, those on the frontiers of social and philosophical thought have no direct connection with those engaged in the daily modification of the human environment: on the one hand, we find abstraction devoid of practice, and on the other practice undignified by reflection. The transformation of the results of pure inquiry in the natural sciences into practical applications escapes the control of the pure scientists: the specialists in transformation—applied scientists and organizational entrepreneurs—are guided by canons of behavior radically different from those of the pure scientists. To complete this description, we have to remind ourselves that pure scientist, social thinker, and artist have little fundamental communication with one another and almost none with the majority of the population. The progressive spread of higher education has not altered this centrifugal tendency in culture, and the possession of a higher educational qualification is of itself no guarantee of access to higher culture. In the circumstances, those who oppose high culture to mass culture miss the point: we have no viable high culture to which to aspire. Rather, we have a discontinuous aggregation of cultures, the contours of which seem to be changing before our eyes, and the future development of which is not foreseeable. The crisis of the universities, in this perspective, is more, and not less, acute.

We must begin with an historical reservation. The responsiveness of the traditional European university to innovation and creation in higher culture has not always been very great. The scholastic stultification of the Sorbonne in the eighteenth century gave rise to a counterculture in the Parisian *salons* and amongst the new bourgeois public, of which the Encyclopedia was the supreme expression. The reforms imposed upon Oxford and Cambridge in the nineteenth century attested the ancient universities' inability to transmit modern culture in any form. Later, the London School of Economics had to be founded to deal with the social sciences. In Germany, sociology—that conspicuous triumph of the early twentieth-century German mind—was only with very great difficulty established as a university discipline. The resistance of university scholars to movements of thought as diverse as Darwinism and psychoanalysis was often extreme. Whole areas of modern cultural creation have grown outside the universities, which have, for instance, been systematically indifferent to much in aesthetic creativity for a century if not longer. Even practical instruction (in applied sciences or the administrative sciences) has often proven impractical, in view of the inability of teachers to assimilate new developments in these fields. Where the universities have been most successful has been in certain fields of pure scientific inquiry,

where criteria of innovation and originality are institutionalized. In the absence of these criteria, or in situations
in which standards of meritorious performance are almost
impossible to objectify (as in the social sciences or humanities) the university offers a telling lesson in the force of
inertia and, often enough, a complacency verging on prej-
udice against the new.

We are witnesses, in a number of countries and in a number of settings, to experiments intended to overcome the
barriers between disciplines. It is sometimes forgotten how
these (entirely admirable) efforts to overcome barriers to
effective inquiry and thought result from the universities'
own tendency to perpetuate unintended arrangements.
The separation of knowledge into distinct disciplines today constitutes a parody of the division of labor found in
the administrative and productive process outside the
university; its historical genesis has rarely been the object
of systematic practical reflection designed to produce a
more viable form for the organization of knowledge. This
is due in part to the persistence of an assumption proper to
the high point of bourgeois culture, that the educated man
could be counted upon to synthesize fragments of knowledge in a personal culture which had both structure and
breadth. Paradoxically, it is also due to the practical ex-
tinction of that assumption. Once knowledge has been fragmented, the road back to a synthesis is impossible to re-
trace, and the effort required itself finds no institutional
framework to support it. It is clear that the present academic division of labor is at times a considerable barrier
to advances in thought and scholarship, in many fields; it
is also clear that these negative impulses to overcome it
may produce provisional solutions to particular difficulties,
but not necessarily anything like a new synthesis. Whether

or not that synthesis is possible, of course, is exceedingly unclear—but it will not be attained unless attempted.

Meanwhile, the universities' relationship to the societies around them has been changing. We may say that the universities once manifested a certain consonance in cultural assumption with the national societies of which they were part, but that consonance rested upon a certain distinctiveness: the universities performed functions which had no equivalent elsewhere and which were not directly integrated with the society's workings. The mode of integration was cultural; the universities formed individuals who took with them into the society the knowledge and sensibility they had acquired in their studies. Consonance with the society has now been replaced by a certain porousness. The universities perform a great many service functions for society, which could in theory and are in fact also accomplished by other agencies (governments, the private sector, independent research establishments). The university professor is not alone the custodian of a distinctive cultural tradition; he is a technical expert, in many instances, whose expertise is indispensable to the accomplishment of society's business. The student is no longer a young adult undergoing initiation into a higher culture. He is a trainee, an educational product whose future productivity is in turn measurable in terms of certain external indices. The use of the language of production and of rationalized administration in discussing universities, increasingly common, expresses the new view of universities as factors in administration and production.

There are those students who bitterly resent the fact that the universities are too well attuned to this world, and those who think that the preparation they are offered is inadequate to its demands. These criticisms fuse in a single perception: that the education given to today's students, given the rate of change of contemporary society, may well be obsolete within ten years of their completing their studies. Differences as to the direction which education should take (whether it should encourage dissidence or prepare the young for assimilation into a social hierarchy unlikely to change in its major dimensions) do not obliterate this common perception. The student's protests, indeed, suggest once again that an ascendant generation is possibly more in touch with the essential requirements of the future than an established one ensconced, if with no great degree of comfort, in what was its own future. Generational dissidence and revolt are not a perpetual social problem, but assume acute forms only under conditions of extreme dissonance between generational experiences. We may ask if the present wave of student revolt in Europe is not positive in its consequences: it has dramatized for the general public a crisis the universities might have preferred to treat within their own walls and at their own speed. We may also ask if, given the rate of cultural change likely to accompany the transition between the next sets of generations, student revolt may not become a permament if periodic aspect of university life—which would of course raise the problem of institutionalizing it. At any rate, it is the very great merit of the discontented student bodies that they have created conditions which make a denial or minimization of the university crisis impossible.

The rapid obsolescence of new knowledge, the recurrent gap between theoretical and practical knowledge, the moral and political choices (insofar as these can in fact be distinguished) entailed in the application of knowledge, all suggest that the European universities would do well to consider a new relationship to praxis. The dangers are obvious. A revulsion for certain kinds of praxis can lead

to the isolation and involution of thought, its academiciza-
tion in a literal and pejorative sense. A fusion with praxis
can lead to an erosion of the distinction between theoretic
and practical knowledge (with, *inter alia,* fatal consequences for the praxis of future generations), a denial of
the critical and imaginative functions of intelligence. That
much said, the present arrangements are largely unten-
able. The relationship between the universities and praxis
is most strictly defined in the older professions (engineering, law, medicine) and even here new professional developments have made basic changes in traditional educational conceptions necessary. The interpenetration of state
and economy, and the invention and utilization of new
techniques of organizational administration and account-
ing, have brought the administration of economic enterprise into the purview of the universities, but the integration with classical instruction in the social sciences of these
new areas of inquiry and instruction remains difficult. A
certain movement between the areas of pure and applied
science is discernible, particularly where governments use
the services of pure scientists on matters of national scientific policy, but this has as yet to find any concrete pedagogic expression in the route education of scientists. Finally, the aesthetic, historical, and reflective disciplines
seem very remote from actuality, quite in contrast with historical periods when abstract disputes were seen to have
concrete political and moral implications.

Possibilities for new relationships to praxis are many,
and these are not exhausted by a certain (and necessary)
modernization of the content of much instruction. That
the film should have equal status as an object of aesthetic
reflection with the novel, that the history of technology
should rank with the history of state systems, that the attention of political philosophy should focus on the conse-

quences of state economic planning rather than be limited to abstract discourse on the good community, are or should be obvious recommendations. Indeed, they are so obvious that they are being put into effect. What is at issue, rather, is the question of the ways in which a new generation can be taught to relate intellectual tradition to concrete social possibility, structures of knowledge to contexts of action. It may well be the case that there is no uniform method for doing so, that the requisite method will vary from discipline to discipline and context to context. Nevertheless, some approach to the problem in a new pedagogic effort is urgent; it is difficult to believe that received methods are adequate to the task.

The question of the introduction of experimental or laboratory methods in instruction may be generalized: is the traditional notion of a temporally integral course of university studies now obsolete? The transmission of the knowledge necessary to forty or forty-five years of occupational activity in three, four, or five years of concentrated educational experience may not be possible. It may be necessary to interrupt occupational activity for repeated and prolonged periods of return to study. Equally, it may be necessary to relate the initial period of higher education to occupational activity (or some form of practical activity) in ways which have as yet been practiced only in disciplines with a specific component of apprenticeship in the career sequences to which they are attached—again, chiefly the professional ones. Briefly, our entire conception of formal higher education may require far more radical emendation than those of us with investments in the traditional methods may care to think. One possible compensation for university teachers, those of the future if not those of the present, may be a very considerable widening of the ranges of experience open in a normal university career.

I have discussed in general and theoretic terms the present relationships amongst the disciplines as precipitates of past efforts to deal with the structure of knowledge and the requirements of instruction, efforts which were appropriate for past phases of university history but which in their present form are rigidified and sometimes senseless. The organizational core of the European university varies: in Germany, the disciplinary institute seems more important than the faculty; in France, the obverse seems true; in Britain, the department dominates the life of the modern universities and the college is still powerful at the ancient universities. Experimental and innovative programs for interdisciplinary work suffer from this disadvantage: those who have begun these programs were often formed in the single disciplines, although the elder innovators have had precisely the advantage of being formed at different and sometimes more open phases of their several disciplines' development. In this setting, the problem of interdisciplinary collaboration is dealt with in order to solve certain concrete problems of inquiry on the frontiers of several disciplines (urban studies in the social sciences, molecular biology in the natural sciences, structural linguistics in the humanities), or in exceedingly general terms, to give a more well rounded education at more elementary levels. Rarely has the notion of a discipline itself, with its connotation of a relatively fixed method of inquiry and of canons of intellectual performance, been examined critically. Modes of interdisciplinary collaboration assume, of course, the existence of disciplines—even if they envisage the emergence of new ones. (The existence of the discipline has been unchallenged in Europe despite the fact that the universities there do educate men who, in later life by no means university teachers, are entirely effective as general intellectuals. It frequently seems that the price of their effectiveness is in fact their location outside the university.) Here, the practical difficulties to be encountered are very great: a programmatic resolve to invent a substitute for the discipline is unlikely to eventuate in any solution susceptible of incorporation in a university organization. The possibilities for organizational innovation here would appear to depend upon a great deal of previous thought, ventures in what may be termed practical epistemology: to what extent and in what ways do advances in thought and inquiry alter the intellectual structures which engendered them? In the meantime, a diversified and intensive pattern of experimentation may heighten the receptivity of the universities to new intellectual structures.

The European universities have had, like universities elsewhere, the most varied functions: the maintenance and transmission of cultural tradition, direct professional preparation, innovation in inquiry and thought. These were formerly accomplished within the unitary framework of universities closely connected with advanced secondary schools (which, it must be remembered, had themselves many of the functions of liberal arts colleges in the United States). A cause (and a result) of the current crisis is the separation of these functions: the contemporary European university is not unlike that of California in meriting the designation "multiversity." It is striking that the university system which seems most acutely affected by the crisis, that of Germany, is the one in which a large number of teachers stubbornly insist on their ability to combine these functions in their own persons. The universities, then, are overburdened and the tasks imposed upon them are not only overwhelming—given the quantitative dimensions of today's demands upon them for teaching and research—but often contradictory. The most obvious solution is the one that has been followed in the United States and which is now being developed, at a very rapid rate indeed, in Europe: the internal differentiation of single institutions to deal with these varied tasks, and the concomitant differentiation of a university system or rather a system of higher education composed of different sorts of institutions, with different sorts of teachers. The obviousness of the solution, and the relative intellectual ease with which traditional administrative arrangements can be thought away (replacing them in practice proves rather more difficult, of course), ought not to obscure the consequence. In the effort to rationalize the functioning of a university suffering from its attempt to do too much (and, very possibly, to do what can no longer be done), the university has lost its contours. I referred to this condition earlier as the porousness of the universities. We may find another term for it, by referring to the functionalization of culture. The new arrangements porposed for the universities integrate them, usually upon the initiative of some form of central scientific and technical planning agency responsive to political considerations, with the present system of social divisions: the universities prepare the upper segment of the labor force for its future tasks, and the internal differentiations within university systems correspond to distinctions within that segment.

The explicit role of the universities in preparing personnel for an indispensable set of social tasks, then, has functionalized culture. The older high bourgeois culture, which assumed that an autonomous intelligence could apprehend and act upon the world as a totality, has disappeared. Philosophy, whose office was once both the pursuit of wisdom and the attainment of synthesis, has detached itself from goals it now considers impossibly old-fashioned and even consummately arrogant. It has become, increasingly, a commentary on the technical operations of the specific disciplines. (This is the claim made in effect for "structuralism" in France, which purports to fuse epistemology and methodology and which in effect reduces the interpretation of history to a decoding operation.) The very idea of discipline, once intended to delimit certain technical procedures for access to different areas of a unified field of knowledge, as changed: a discipline is no longer a means of access to reality but a partial definition of an autonomous reality. In the circumstances, it is not surprising that the universities have renounced as impractical or unattainable the central intellectual tasks of our epoch. The bridging of the abyss between the natural sciences and the humanities, the rethinking of the status and limits of the newer social sciences and their relationship to the historical disciplines, the adjudication of conflict between technological immanence and human purpose, have all gone by default. Alternatively, they have been allocated to the reserved domain of "social critics" whose academic status consists precisely in the fact that they have none, that they are outside the "professional" world of the separate disciplines. By one of those historical ironies which are familiar to our epoch, society's immediate demands upon the universities, their porousness to the outside world, and the functionalization of the culture they mediate have reduced their long-term ability to shape that world. The elites shaped by the contemporary universities know much, but they do not know how much they ignore. The idea of a functionally specific university system, preparing with sociological exactitude the cadres for the new bureaucratic oligarchy, for the intermediate and subordinate echelons of the new administrative and productive systems, in fact constitutes an adjustment of elite preparation to a temporary phase of the organization of culture and society. The contemporaneity of the university condemns it to a rapid technological obsolescence.

Are there any possibilities, then, that the European universities might recover their ancient inner unity? It is more plausible to ask if there are any possibilities that they can develop a new form of unity, with a new content.

It is at this point that we enter the realm of sociological speculation. The pedagogic practices of the European universities have proven defective, and the consciousness of this amongst university teachers in Europe is very great. Nevertheless, the final form and content of any reform programs now embarked upon will depend not alone upon the consciousness of the universities but equally upon the ability of critical university teachers to find allies amongst elites outside the universities. Enough has been said here and elsewhere to suggest that the character of those elites is changing: bureaucratic and technical qualifications (even in the sphere of politics and administration) are beginning to replace the inheritance of property and the mastery of a general culture become increasingly ornamental. It will be remembered that the universities were supreme agencies, in the nineteenth century, for the completion of the transition between the fused aristocratic and bourgeois culture of the preindustrial epoch and the bourgeois culture of the early industrial period. They became, with no clear philosophical justification available (Max Weber's "Wissenschaft als Beruf" ("Science as a Vocation") was a despairing acknowledgment of the fact), training centers for the new elites—all the time retaining as legitimations the older and now antiquated notions of general culture. It may be asked whether the gradual accession to power of new social types may bring with it not alone the usual requirements for a justificatory ideology (which some in the universities have in any case not been slow to invent) but also the demand for new intellectual and cultural syntheses. The increasing perfection of technique and the increasing rationalization of administration pose problems not resoluble in terms of the education now available to those exercising the new sorts of power, because these are problems which concern the historical and moral context of technique and administration rather than their immanent development. The relative success of socialist beliefs amongst bourgeois university teachers in some countries (notably Britain and France) in the first half of this century was due to the conviction of many on the frontiers of bourgeois thought that the assumptions under which they had been educated were no longer valid. They sought an alliance, therefore, with the political and moral force they thought represented by the working-class movement, which in turn required the intellectual and moral force lent to it by those in command of bourgeois culture. The new technocratic elite and the new technical intelligentsia may well require cultural and intellectual resources not now accessible to it. The very obsolescence of those remnants of traditional high culture found in the universities may render some university teachers more willing to experiment with new alliances, and to see in the present crisis not only the destruction of an older culture but the chance to develop a newer one. Whether a new technological humanism can emerge depends not least on the ability of the universities to detach themselves from some of the immediate demands of a technological epoch, to form new alliances, and to risk being wrong (or worse, derided or ignored). I have said that an alliance with those exercising new types of power would constitute a first step toward a new definition of general culture for the universities, but an alliance requires a certain equality amongst allies. Insofar as the universities define themselves as functional appendages of the new elites, or simply as part of them, no independent contribution to that definition from the universities can be expected. Not the least of the tasks confronting the European universities is that of reinventing a critical general consciousness. That the culture outside the universities seems able to dispense with that consciousness is no necessary indication that it has no historical function to fulfill.

The path to a general consciousness, however, must lie in the solution of particular, often concrete, problems. More of the European universities will have to show some of the willingness to experiment shown by some of their American sister institutions. Curricular experiments in the incorporation of humanistic and social scientific perspectives in the education of scientists and technologists, political philosophical instruction for those preparing for administrative and managerial careers, natural scientific and technological instruction for humanists and social scientists, are necessary: these are possible only insofar as those on the frontiers of the disciplines make the effort to redefine their own perspectives. That intellectual redefinition in turn can come only through a new view of the functions of the university, and this may well entail a new conception of its relationship to society. The previous remoteness of the European university has gone and has been replaced by a sublime form of intellectual servitude. A newer, or greater, freedom to deal on terms of equality with new elites may come if the universities increase their contacts with other and more disadvantaged groups in the population: the idea of universities as centers of popular education has in this respect much to recommend it, and should appeal to university teachers distrustful of the encroachments of mass culture in European society. Finally, as university teachers attempt to define new subject matters and new pedagogical techniques, new organizational forms for the university will become imperative. The rethinking of a certain isolation from practical activity is urgent; equally so is a new view of the role of the student in the university structure, and indeed, if the age and occupational experience of student bodies increases, that new view will become easier to develop. It will be seen that the European universities do not lack possibilities for solutions to the crisis which racks them at the moment. If, however, pedagogic and organizational reform is attempted without new efforts to think about their role, about the structure and future of higher culture itself, the crisis will hardly be surmounted.

VIII

The task imposed on the universities may well prove too strenuous, and the development of a new culture unifying technique and meaning will probably have to await the groping efforts of generations. For the moment, we may say that industrial culture (whatever its religious roots) has forced men to confront a world emptied of transcendence. The ineluctable progression of science and technology, the objectification of culture in processes seemingly (and for millions, actually) autonomous of human will, the increasing disparity between mankind's cognitive resources and its capacity to create viable communities (much less a single human community), have combined to erode the cognitive bases of religious belief. The shrunken and battered authority and relevance of the family, the immeasurably reduced importance of local and primary institutions, have undermined the psychological foundations on which all historical religions have rested. In these circumstances, the efforts of the churches to find new forms of mission in industrial society entail the acceptance by the ecclesiastical avant-garde (which has much in common, in age and outlook, with the political avant-garde described in the previous chapter) of the process of secularization.

The churches, in the persons of those who constitute their spiritual elites, are attempting to take root in a culture made by men but curiously resistant to humanizing purposes. What of ordinary men and women, deprived (apart from ritual obeisance and formal adhesion to the churches) of the traditional forms of religiosity? The hopes of those eighteenth- and nineteenth-century prophets who envisaged a matured humanity, one which could emerge from the supposed infantilism of religion, have been disappointed. New forms of submission and psychological repression, new regressions, have replaced the older ones. Freud, a prophet despite himself, supposed that psychoanalysis would constitute a new spiritual discipline for mankind—of a liberating kind. The most cursory examination of industrial culture suggests that liberation is distant. A great nineteenth-century critic of religion, the ex-priest Loisy, once declared that men had expected the kingdom of God and had instead experienced the Catholic Church. We may state that men had looked forward to their inner and outer freedom; instead, psychological illumination has ended in market research.

I have written above of the cleft in culture caused by the increasing isolation of family and community from the major political and cultural processes. The conservatives have deplored the loss of familial authority (and from Comte to the late Stalin have sought to restore it); radicals have applauded it. Its cultural consequences still require examination. It is easy enough to speak, with many sociologists, of the transfer to other agencies (schools, work groups, the media of mass communication) of the family's functions of psychological discipline and moral education. The consequence, the subjection of the individual to a continuing process of socialization, the continual bombardment of the human person by directives, has drastically altered the fact as well as the notion of personality. David Riesman has described the "other directed personality"—but it might be more accurate to say that the "other directed personality" is in no very discernible sense a personality at all. At any rate, the retention of the form of the family combines with its obvious loss of function to render our present familial institutions peculiarly vulnerable. The familiar phenomena of late industrial cultures, early physical maturity and increasingly early sexuality, the socialization of children by peer groups (themselves often manipulated by the mass media and in this sense not autonomous or spontaneous), institutionalized generational conflict, are connected with these changes in what was once the primary social institution.

The family's role as the single permitted site of sexuality, a fundament of bourgeois legitimacy for centuries, is in equal disrepair. It does not follow that satisfactory solutions to the problem of sexuality have been found. The flood of pronouncements, publications, and inquiries on this subject do give the impression that some of our contemporaries have the idea that they are the first human generation to discover the existence of a distinction between the sexes. It is surprising that so little of this discussion has been connected with the social and cultural role of women, who to some extent remain an oppressed group in industrial societies with bourgeois heritages. (The occupational distribution statistics show that the "emancipation" of American middle-class women is no emancipation at all. In the recent expansion of the university-educated population, and despite the need for persons with advanced degrees, the proportion of women doing postgraduate study has actually declined. American middle-class women are, perhaps, so strident and so domineering precisely because they have in the last analyses neither influence nor power.) In the midst of this general decomposition, it is not surprising that recent innovations in style of dress and comportment by the young express a confusion, or fusion—the term seems at this point an arbitrary matter—of sexes. Whether the liberties taken by the newer generation can be institutionalized as they grow older remains a question.

The rift between family, community and the dominant social processes (those of administration and production) constitutes a problem in culture for two reasons. The most obvious one is that it poses severe problems of interpretation and symbolic consonance to those whose lives are riven by this discontinuity. The second reason subsumes the first and gives it a psychological structure—if a structure itself rent by conflicts. I have evoked, however briefly, the problems of personality, instinctual expression (or sexuality) and family to suggest that the crisis of industrial culture has had a deforming effect on primordial human functions. Not alone does the organization of industrial culture in its present apparatus deny to men the possibility of comprehending the whole, let alone utilizing or mastering it. It also represses their energies, denies them instinctual satisfactions, blocks their imaginations. In short, it creates the psychological conditions which make a new humanization of culture seem impossible, since it makes the concrete transcendence of the present appear utopian.

If a human community of mastery, liberty, and delight appears utopian, we are entitled to turn in our search for a way toward it, to those who in industrial culture have for a century and a half practiced a concrete utopia. The artists have existed at times near the center, more often on the margins, of industrial existence. Even those (like William Morris or LeCorbusier and the entire group involved in the modern movement in plastic art) who have attempted to find new aesthetic forms derived from industrial experience have found it difficult to communicate with those at the center of that experience. Not industrial workers but the bourgeoisie, not engineers but those with humanistic educations, have responded to the modern movement. One aspect in particular of artistic creation since the industrial revolution is singular: its encapsulation, by and large, in communities of artists (whether plastic or literary). In particular, in those communities known as bohemian the artists not only found the support of their peers but an immediately responsive, if small, public. They engaged, not always consciously, in experimentation with a new style of life. They were free of routine, if not of material worries, and often enough disrespectful of bourgeois convention.

The bohemian communities of Europe developed in its cities in the nineteenth century. They were augmented, as time went on, by large numbers of students—often temporary bohemians, who later settled for bourgeois careers. A certain largesse of view, above all in the treatment of time, marked their descent from aristocratic traditions. In a sense, we may interpret the bohemians as continuing in bourgeois society an aristocratic habit: fashioning a style of life remote from the actual processes of material production. The bohemians for much of the modern period have been on the frontiers of cultural consciousness: the symbolist poets anticipated psychoanalysis, and the first abstract artists seemed to sense the coming of new concepts of space and time. Marx himself praised Balzac as having depicted, implacably, the mechanisms of the market and their consequences for human personality.

The work of the bohemians, of course, has been assimilated to ordinary consciousness—usually after an interval sufficient to blunt its critical impact. Mondrian's forms, once dismissed by a bourgeois public irritated at their lack of literalism, now mark the graphic arts—not least in advertising. We are now, indeed, at a point at which the work of the aesthetic avant-garde has immediate marketability. In these circumstances, genuine innovation and sheer sensationalism, critical acuity with respect to ordinary perception and cynical titillation of a satiated public, seem hopelessly mixed. The present vogue of pop art, where it is not simply fraudulent, attests the limits of this situation. Pop art, a bastard offspring of the modern movement, makes no pretense of transcending the fragmentation and senselessness of perception in industrial culture. Pop art entails a simultaneous satiric rejection of popular culture and high culture. It has broken with the reflective and interpretative functions of art. Experience now knows nothing outside its own surface or, rather, the most insistently trivial dimensions of its own surface appearance. Those who through pop art laugh at popular culture accept its frame of reference. They have renounced their own integration with cultural tradition and accepted their imprisonment within an historical moment organized about its own meaningless and ephemeral quality. This implicit attack on high art and high culture is a pseudo-revolutionary phenomenon—a revolution for philistines. It is also an expression of the failure of the "educated" to educate themselves in sensibility of spiritual effort.

Bohemianism, then, seems to have been on the verge of capitulation to industrial society's apparent capacity to nullify any form of dissent. New developments, however, show that it has surprising political force. In some of the state socialist countries, particularly in the Soviet Union, bohemianism—outside the sanctioned and controlled institutions of public culture—has criminal status. Free aesthetic creation and moral experimentation do seem to contravene a "socialist art" and a "socialist morality" characterized by rigidity, repression, and ineradicable dullness. In the "liberal" industrial regimes, the rebirth of bohemianism has been the work of the young. The proliferation in America and Europe of "hippie" communities expressed the refusal of routine by many destined for safe careers. These communities have been isolated from the main currents of politics, and it is not surprising that many of their members turned to drugs: there seemed to be no way in which, apart from inner ecstasy or withdrawal from the world, their critique of routine could find institutional expression. Intimations of the politicization of bohemia, and above all of its younger adherents, have not been lacking. The French Revolution of May 1968 showed the explosive force of the union of bohemianism with radical politics. "L'imagination au pouvoir!" ("All power to the imagination") was the cry of the first phase of this revolution, in the Latin Quarter—an interesting contrast with the "All power to the Soviets" of 1917.

The younger workers who (to the astonishment of the French trade union bureaucrats) came to the Latin Quarter to support the students against the police and then launched the occupation of the factories were remote from high culture. However, both students and workers shared in that mass movement of cultural innovation which began a decade ago amongst working class and bourgeois youth in Europe. The emergence of groups of pop artists, of self-entertainment amongst the young, modified the pattern of commercial exploitation of the popular arts. For once, these were made by the people (or some of them) instead of for them. Absolute domination of the cultural market by the sellers changed into a frantic pursuit of the tastes of new buyers. The Beatles in England; the young *chansonniers* like Antoine in France; Bob Dylan and Joan Baez in America, had this in common: they spoke not alone of immediate and private concerns but they gave these general accents. They dealt with parents and bosses, with the atomic bomb and politicians. The entire new generation did experiment with new forms for its own sensibilities, and they were critical of an elder generation which seemed to demand only compliance with an unrewarding routine. For once, mass culture had as its content neither total escape from routine or an ignoble capitulation to it, but a modicum of criticism of it. The barricades erected by the Parisian students had, apparently, symbolic value for an entire generation.

Some of the points of contact between the students and workers are obvious. Both were incensed at the authoritarianism and gerontocracy of the institutions in which they found themselves. Both had good reason to doubt that they would find employment consonant with their capacities or education. (The younger workers had acquired advanced technical skills ignored in their factories.) The workers had no experience of high culture, but high culture in its parental or university form struck the students—to judge by their own testimony—as irrelevant and lifeless. It is certainly true that the May Revolution was a temporary union of those who refused the "consumer society" (a phrase much used in those days) and those who did not consume enough. The absurdity and inhumanity of a society organized precisely about this difference obsessed the participants.

In the chiliastic atmosphere generated by the astonishing initial success of the revolution, both the students and the younger workers had recourse to modes of expression and comportment available only in bohemia. The Ecole des Beaux-Arts, or rather its students, played an immensely important visual role in the revolution. An outburst of spontaneity resulted in caricature and laughter, analysis and satire, promulgated on the walls of classrooms and factories, in a hundred new newspapers and thousands of pamphlets. André Malraux, who has a considerable experience of revolution, was moved to declare that the alliance of students and workers constituted a crisis of civilization. The demand for autonomy, the attack on paternalism and bureaucracy, above all the young revolutionaries' insistence that work and pleasure be fused, did voice a profound revulsion for industrial culture in its present form. The revolution itself, however, gives hope that industrial culture can be humanized if men again take power into their own hands. A series of revolutions will be needed before *Homo faber* can be reborn. Under conditions of high technological development, the revolutionary role of art is striking. Instead of art reflecting life, life itself is beginning to express the freedom hitherto reserved for art.

BIBLIOGRAPHY

THE BIBLIOGRAPHY gives an indication, not entirely complete, of the sources I have drawn upon. Although the text has not been altered since 1968, I have added some recent titles bearing on the argument. Wherever possible, I have cited English translations in addition to the original French or German.

Abendroth, Wolfgang. *Sozialgeschichte der europäischen Arbeiterbewegung.* (3. Aufl.) Frankfurt: Suhrkamp, 1966.
——. *Antagonistische Gesellschaft und politische Demokratie.* Neuwied: Luchterhand, 1967.
——, et al. *Die Linke antwortet Jürgen Habermas.* Frankfurt: Europaische Verlagsanstalt, 1968.
Adorno, Theodor. *Minima Moralia.* Berlin: Suhrkamp, 1951.
Althusser, Louis. *Pour Marx.* Paris: F. Maspero, 1966.
Anderson, Perry, and Blackburn, Robin (eds.) *Towards Socialism.* London: Collins, 1966.
Aron, Raymond. *La Sociologie allemande contemporaine.* Paris: F. Alcan, 1935.
——. *German Sociology,* trans. by Mary and Thomas Bottomore. London: Heinemann, 1957.
——. *L'Opium des intellectuels.* Paris: Calmann-Lévy, 1955.
——. *The Opium of the Intellectuals,* trans. by Terence Kilmartin. Garden City, N. Y.: Doubleday, 1957.
——. *Dix-huit leçons sur la société industrielle.* Paris: Gallimard, 1962.

———. *18 Lectures on Industrial Society*. London: Weidenfeld and Nicolson, 1969.

———. *La lutte de classes*. Paris: Gallimard, 1964.

———. *Trois essais sur l'âge industriel*. Paris: Plon, 1965.

———. *The Industrial Society*. New York: Praeger, 1967.

———. *Démocratie et totalitarianisme*. Paris: Gallimard, 1965.

———. *Democracy and Totalitarianism*, trans. by Valence Ionescu. London: Weidenfeld and Nicolson, 1968.

———. *La révolution introuvable*. Paris: Fayard, 1968.

Bahrdt, Hans Paul. *Industriebürokratie*. Stuttgart: Enke, 1958.

Bazelon, David. *Power in America*. New York: New American Library, 1967.

———. *Nothing But a Fine Tooth Comb*. New York: Simon and Schuster, 1969.

Beard, Charles A. *An Economic Interpretation of the Constitution of the United States*. New York: Macmillan, 1913.

———, and Mary. *America in Midpassage*. New York: Macmillan, 1939.

Bell, Daniel. *The End of Ideology*. Glencoe: Free Press, 1960.

———. "Notes on the Post-Industrial Society," I and II, *The Public Interest*, Nos. 6 and 7 (Winter 1966, and Spring 1967).

Ben-David, Joseph. "Professions in the Class System of Present-Day Societies," *Current Sociology*, Vol. 12, No. 3, 1963-64.

Bendix, Reinhard. *Work and Authority in Industry*. New York: Wiley, 1956.

———. *Nation-building and Citizenship*. New York: Wiley, 1964.

———, and Lipset, S. M. (eds.) *Class, Status and Power*. (2d ed.). New York: Free Press, 1966.

Benjamin, Walter. *Kunstwerk im Zeitalter seiner technischen Reproduzierbarkeit*. Berlin: Suhrkamp, 1963.

Bensman, Joseph, *Dollars and Sense*. New York: Macmillan, 1967.

Bergmann, Uwe; Dutschke, Rudi; Lefèvre, Wolfgang; and Rabehl, Bernd. *Rebellion der Studenten oder die neue Opposition*. Hamburg: Rowoholt, 1968.

Berle, Adolph A. *Power without Property*. New York: Harcourt, Brace, 1959.

———, and Means, Gardiner C. *The Modern Corporation and Private Property*. New York: Macmillan, 1933.

Barnstein, Barton (ed.) *Towards a New Past*. New York: Pantheon, 1968.

Birnbaum, Norman. "The Sociological Analysis of Ideology, 1940-60," *Current Sociology*, Vol. 9, No. 2, 1960. (Oxford: Blackwell's, 1962, and New York: Johnson Reprint Corporation, 1965).

————, and Lenzer, Gertrud (eds.) *Sociology and Religion*. Englewood Cliffs, N. J.: Prentice-Hall, 1968.

Bloch, Ernst. *Religion im Erbe*. Frankfurt: Suhrkamp, 1966.

————. *Man on His Own*, trans. by E. B. Ashton. New York: Herder and Herder, 1970.

Bon, Frédéric, and Burnier, Michel-Antoine. *Les Nouveaux Intellectuels*. Paris: Cujas, 1966.

Borkenau, Franz. *Übergang von Feudalen zum bürgerlichen Weltbild*. Paris: F. Alcan, 1934.

Bottomore, Thomas B. *Elites and Society*. London: Watts, 1964.

————. *Classes in Modern Society*. New York: Pantheon, 1966.

Bourdieu, Pierre, and Passeron, Jean-Claude. *Les héritiers*. Paris: Editions de Minuit, 1964.

Chomsky, Noam. *American Power and the New Mandarins*. New York: Pantheon, 1969.

Clapham, J. H. *The Economic Development of France and Germany 1815-1914*. (4th ed.) Cambridge, England: The University Press, 1936.

Cockburn, Alexander, and Blackburn, Robin (eds.) *Student Power*. London: Penguin, 1969.

Cohn-Bendit, Daniel and Gabriel. *Le gauchisme. Remède à la maladie sénile du communisme*. Paris: Seuil, 1968.

————. *Obsolete Communism: The Left-Wing Alternative*, trans. by Arnold Pomerans. New York: McGraw-Hill, 1969.

Commons, John R. *Legal Foundations of Capitalism*. New York: Macmillan, 1924.

Comte, Auguste. *Cours de philosophie positive*. (6 vols.) Paris: Bachelier, 1830-42.

————. *The Positive Philosophy*, trans. and condensed by Harriet Martineau. London: Chapman, 1869.

————. *Système de politique positive*. (4 vols.) Paris: L. Mathias, 1851-54.

──────. *System of Positive Polity,* trans. by John Henry Bridges. (4 vols.) London: Longmans, Green, 1875-77.

Crosland, C. A. R. *The Future of Socialism.* London: J. Cape, 1956.

Dahl, Robert A. *A Preface to Democratic Theory.* Chicago: University of Chicago Press, 1956.

──────. *Who Governs?* New Haven: Yale University Press, 1961.

Dahrendorf, Ralf. *Class and Class Conflict in Industrial Society.* Stanford: Stanford University Press, 1959.

──────. *Gesellschaft und Freiheit.* München: R. Piper, 1962.

──────. *Essays in the Theory of Society,* trans. by the author. Stanford: Stanford University Press, 1968.

──────. *Gesellschaft und Demokratie in Deutschland.* Munich: Piper, 1965.

──────. *Society and Democracy in Germany,* trans. by the author. Garden City, N.Y.: Doubleday, 1967.

Debord, Guy. *La Société de spectacle.* Paris: Buchet/Chastel, 1967.

Debray, Régis. *Révolution dans la révolution?* Paris: F. Maspero, 1967.

──────. *Revolution in the Revolution?* trans. by Bobbye Ortis. New York: Grove Press, 1967.

Desroche, Henri. *Socialismes et sociologie religieuse.* Paris: Cujas, 1965.

──────. *Sociologie des religions.* Paris: P.U.F., 1969.

Djilas, Milovan. *The New Class.* New York: Praeger, 1957.

Dupeux, Georges. *La Société française, 1789-1960.* (2d ed.) Paris: A. Colin, 1964.

Erikson, Erik. *Childhood and Society.* New York: Norton, 1950.

──────. *Young Man Luther.* New York: Norton, 1958.

──────. *Identity: Youth and Crisis.* New York: Norton, 1968.

Etzioni, Amitai. *The Active Society.* New York: Free Press, 1968.

Ferguson, Adam. *An Essay on the History of Civil Society, 1767.* Edinburgh: University Press, 1966.

Fourastié, Jean. *Les 40,000 heures.* Paris: R. Laffont, 1965.

Francastel, Pierre. *Art et technique.* Paris: Gonthier, 1964.

Freud, Sigmund. *Totem und Tabu.* Wien: Heller, 1913.

──────. *Totem and Taboo,* trans. by J. Strachey. London: Routledge, 1919.

──────. *Massenpsychologie und Ich-Analyse.* Leipzig: Internationaler Psychoanalytischer Verlag, 1921.

————. *Group Psychology and the Analysis of the Ego,* trans. by J. Strachey. London: International Psychoanalytical Press, 1922.

————. *Das Unbehagen in der Kultur.* Wien: Internationaler Psychoanalytischer Verlag, 1930.

————. *Civilization and Its Discontents,* trans. by J. Riviere. London: Hogarth Press, 1930.

Friedmann, Georges. *Problèmes humains du machinisme industriel.* Paris: Gallimard, 1946.

————. *Industrial Society: the Emergence of the Human Problem of Automatioπ,* trans. by John Spaulding, Mary and Tom Bottomore; ed. and intro. by Harold L. Sheppard. Glencoe: Free Press, 1955.

————. *Où va le travail humain?* (rev. ed.) Paris: Gallimard, 1960.

————. *Anatomy of Work,* trans. by Wyatt Rawson. New York: Free Press, 1961.

————. *Sept études sur l'homme et la technique.* Paris: Gonthier, 1966.

Galbraith, John Kenneth. *American Capitalism.* Boston: Houghton Mifflin, 1956.

————. *The Affluent Society.* Boston: Houghton Mifflin, 1958.

————. *The New Industrial State.* Boston: Houghton Mifflin, 1967.

Garaudy, Roger. *Le grand tournant du socialisme.* Paris: Gallimard, 1969.

Geiger, Theodor. *Arbeiten zur Soziologie.* Neuwied: Luchterhand, 1962.

Gellner, Ernest. *Thought and Change.* Chicago: University of Chicago Press, 1964.

Glass, David V. (ed.) *Social Mobility in Britain.* London: Routledge and Paul, 1954.

Goldmann, Lucien. *Recherches dialectiques.* (3d ed.) Paris: Gallimard, 1959.

————. *Le Dieu caché.* Paris: Gallimard, 1955.

————. *The Hidden God,* trans. by P. Thody. New York: Humanities Press, 1964.

————. *Pour une sociologie de roman.* Paris: Gallimard, 1964.

Goldthorpe, John; Lockwood, David; Bechofer, Frank; and Platt, Jennifer. *The Affluent Worker.* (3 vols.) London: Cambridge University Press, 1968.

Gorz, André. *Stratégie ouvrière et néo-capitalisme.* Paris: Seuil, 1964.

————. *Strategy for Labor,* trans. by Martin A. Nicolaus and Victoria Ortiz. Boston: Beacon, 1967.

————. *Le socialisme difficile.* Paris: Seuil, 1967.

Grana, César. *Bohemian versus Bourgeois.* New York: Basic Books, 1964.

Graubard, Stephen R. (ed.) *A New Europe?* Boston: Houghton Mifflin, 1964.

Grundriss der Sozialökonomik. (IX. Abteilung, 1. Teil) Tübingen: Mohr, 1926.

Gurvitch, Georges. *La Vocation actuelle de la sociologie.* Paris: P.U.F., 1950.

————. *Le Concept de classe social, de Marx à nos jours.* Paris: C.D.U., 1954.

————. *Déterminismes sociaux et liberté humaine.* Paris: P.U.F., 1955.

Habermas, Jürgen. *Strukturwandel der Oeffentlichkeit.* Neuwied: Luchterhand, 1962.

————. *Theorie und Praxis.* Neuwied: Luchterhand, 1963.

———— (ed.) *Antworten auf Herbert Marcuse.* Frankfurt: Suhrkamp, 1968.

————. *Protestbewegung und Hochschulreform.* Frankfurt: Suhrkamp, 1969.

————. *Technik und Wissenschaft als "Ideologie".* Frankfurt: Suhrkamp, 1969.

Harrington, Michael. *The Accidental Century.* New York: Macmillan, 1965.

————. *Towards a Democratic Left.* New York: Macmillan, 1968.

Hauser, Arnold. *The Social History of Art.* (2 vols.) New York: Knopf, 1951.

————. *Sozialgeschichte der Kunst und Literatur.* (2 vols.) München: H. Beck, 1953.

Hazard, Paul. *La Crise de la conscience européene.* Paris: Bovin, 1935.

————. *The European Mind, the Critical Years, 1680-1715,* trans. by J. Lewis May. New Haven: Yale University Press, 1953.

Heberle, Rudolf. *Social Movements.* New York: Appleton-Century-Crofts, 1951.

Heer, Friederich. *Mittelalter.* Zürich: Kindler, 1961.

————. *The Medieval World,* trans. by J. Sondheimer. Cleveland: World, 1962.

Heilbroner, Robert L. *The Quest for Wealth*. New York: Simon and Schuster, 1956.

———. *The Future as History*. New York: Harper, 1960.

———. *The Making of Economic Society*. Englewood Cliffs, N. J.: Prentice-Hall, 1962.

———. *The Great Ascent*. New York: Harper and Row, 1963.

———. *The Limits of American Capitalism*. New York: Harper and Row, 1966.

Heller, Celia S. (ed.) *Structured Social Inequality*. New York: Macmillan, 1969.

Hill, Christopher. *Puritanism and Revolution*. London: Secker and Warburg, 1958.

———. *Intellectual Origins of the English Revolution*. Oxford: Clarendon Press, 1965.

Hobsbawn, Eric. *The Age of Revolution 1789-1848*. London: Weidenfeld and Nicolson, 1962.

———. *Labouring Men*. London: Weidenfeld and Nicolson, 1964.

———. *Industry and Empire*. London: Weidenfeld and Nicolson, 1968.

Hofstadter, Richard. *The American Political Tradition and the Men Who Made It*. New York: Knopf, 1951.

———. *The Age of Reform*. New York: Knopf, 1956.

———. *Anti-Intellectualism in American Life*. New York: Knopf, 1963.

Holz, Hans Heinz. "Die verschleierte Klassengesellschaft" in Kruger, Horst (ed.) *Was ist heute Links?* Munich: List Verlag, 1963.

Horkheimer, Max. *The Eclipse of Reason*. New York: Oxford University Press, 1947.

———. *Kritische Theorie*. I and II. Frankfurt: Suhrkamp, 1968.

———, and Adorno, Theodor. *Dialektik der Aufklaerung*. Amsterdam: Querido, 1947.

Howe, Irving. *Politics and the Novel*. Cleveland: World, 1957.

———. *Steady Work*. New York: Harcourt, Brace and World, 1966.

Institut für Sozialforschung. *Soziologische Exkurse*. Frankfurt: Europäische Verlagsanstalt, 1956.

Isambert, François-André. *Christianisme et classe ouvrière*. Tournai-Paris: Casterman, 1961.

Jantke, Carl. *Der vierte Stand*. Frieburg: Herder, 1955.

Joll, James. *Intellectuals in Politics*. London: Weidenfeld and Nicolson, 1960.

Kaplan, Morton A. (ed.) *The Revolution in World Politics.* New York: Wiley, 1962.

Keniston, Kenneth. *Young Radicals.* New York: Harcourt, Brace and World, 1968.

Kogon, Eugen. *Der SS-Staat.* München: K. Alber, 1946.

————. *Theory and Practise of Hell,* trans. by Heinz Norden. New York: Farrar, Straus, 1950.

Kolakowski, Leszek. *Der Mensch ohne Alternative.* München R. Piper, 1961.

————. *Toward a Marxist Humanism,* trans. by Jane Zielonko Peel. New York: Grove Press, 1968.

Kolko, Gabriel. *Wealth and Power in America.* New York: Praeger, 1962.

Lane, Robert. *Political Ideology.* New York: Free Press, 1962.

Lasch, Christopher. *The Agony of the American Left.* New York: Knopf, 1969.

Lazarsfeld, Marie Jahoda, *et al. Die Arbeitslosen von Marienthal.* Leipzig: S. Hirzel, 1933.

Lazarsfeld, Paul. *The People's Choice.* New York: Duell, Sloan and Pearce, 1944.

————, *et al. Voting.* Chicago: University of Chicago Press, 1954.

Lederer, Emil. *State of the Masses.* New York: Norton, 1940.

Lefebvre, Henri. *Critique de la vie quotidienne. (2* vols., 2d ed.) Paris: L'Arche, 1958–62.

————. *La Somme et le reste.* (2 vols.) Paris: La Nef de Paris, 1959.

————. *Métaphilosophie.* Paris: Editions de Minuit, 1965.

————. *Positions: contre les technocrates.* Paris: Gonthier, 1967.

————. *L'Irruption.* Paris: Editions Anthropos, 1968.

————. *Le Droit à la ville.* Paris: Editions Anthropos, 1968.

Le Play, F. *Les ouvriers européens.* Paris: Imprimerie impériale, 1855.

Levin, Murray. *The Alienated Voter.* New York: Holt, Rinehart and Winston, 1960.

Lichtheim, George. *Marxism; an Historical and Critical Study.* New York: Praeger, 1961.

————. *The New Europe.* New York: Praeger, 1963.

————. *Marxism in Modern France.* New York: Columbia University Press, 1966.

————. *The Concept of Ideology and Other Essays.* New York: Vintage, 1967.

Lipset, Seymour Martin. *Political Man.* Garden City: Doubleday, 1960.

——. *The First New Nation.* New York: Basic Books, 1963.

——, and Bendix, Reinhard. *Social Mobility in Industrial Society.* Berkeley: University of California Press, 1959.

Lockwood, David. *The Black-Coated Worker.* London: Allen and Unwin, 1958.

Lukacs, György. *Geschichte und Klassenbewusstein.* Berlin: Malik, 1923.

Lynd, Robert S. *Knowledge for What.* Princeton: Princeton University Press, 1939.

——, and Helen M. *Middletown.* New York: Harcourt, Brace, 1929.

McKenzie, Robert T. *British Political Parties.* London: Heinemann, 1955.

MacPherson, C. B. *The Political Theory of Possessive Individualism: Hobbes to Locke.* Oxford: Clarendon Press, 1962.

MacQuarrie, John. *Twentieth-century Religious Thought.* New York: Harper and Row, 1963.

Mallet, Serge. *Les Paysans contre le passé.* Paris: Seuil, 1962.

——. *La nouvelle classe ouvrière.* Paris: Seuil, 1963.

——. *Gaullisme et la gauche.* Paris: Seuil, 1965.

Mandel, Ernest. *Traité d'économie marxiste.* Paris: Julliard, 1962.

——. *Marxist Economic Theory,* trans. by Brian Pearce. (2 vols.) New York: Monthly Review Press, 1968.

Mannheim, Karl. *Mensch und Gesellschaft im Zeitalter des Umbaus.* Leiden: Sijthoff's, 1935.

——. *Man and Society in an Age of Reconstruction,* trans. by Edward Shils. London: Kegan Paul, 1940.

——. *Ideologie und Utopie.* 3. Vermehrte Auflage. Frankfurt: Schulte-Bulmke, 1952.

——. *Ideology and Utopia,* trans. by Louis Wirth and Edward Shils. New York: Harcourt, Brace, 1936.

Marcuse, Herbert. *Reason and Revolution.* London: Oxford University Press, 1941.

——. *Eros and Civilization.* Boston: Beacon Press, 1955.

——. *One-Dimensional Man.* Boston: Beacon Press, 1964.

——. *An Essay on Liberation.* Boston: Beacon Press, 1969.

——; Moore, Barrington; and Wolf, Robert Paul. *Repressive Tolerance.* (2d ed.). Boston: Beacon Press, 1969.

Mead, Margaret. *Culture and Commitment*. New York: Doubleday, 1970.

Merton, Robert K. *Social Theory and Social Structure*. (rev., enlarged ed.) New York: Free Press, 1957.

Miliband, Ralph. *Parliamentary Socialism*. London: Allen and Unwin, 1961.

————. *The State in Capitalist Society*. London: Weidenfeld and Nicolson, 1968.

Millar, John. *Observations Concerning the Distinction of Ranks in Society*. London: John Murray, 1771.

Miller, S. M., and Rein, M. "Poverty, Inequality and Policy" in Becker, Howard S. (ed.) *Social Problems*. New York: Wiley, 1966.

Miller, S. M., and Riessman, Frank. *Social Class and Social Policy*. New York: Basic Books, 1968.

Mills, C. Wright. *The New Men of Power*. New York: Harcourt, Brace, 1948.

————. *White Collar*. New York: Oxford, 1951.

————. *The Power Elite*. New York: Oxford, 1956.

————. *The Sociological Imagination*. New York: Oxford, 1959.

————. *Power, Politics and People*. New York: Oxford, 1963.

Mitscherlich, Alexander. *Auf dem Weg zur vaterlosen Gesellschaft*. München: R. Piper, 1963.

Moltmann, Jürgen. *Theologie der Hoffnung*. München: Kaiser, 1966.

————. *Theology of Hope*, trans. by James W. Leitch. New York: Harper and Row, 1967.

Moore, Barrington, Jr. *Soviet Politics*. Cambridge: Harvard University Press, 1950.

————. *Terror and Progress USSR*. Cambridge: Harvard University Press, 1954.

————. *Social Origins of Dictatorship and Democracy*. Boston: Beacon Press, 1966.

Morazé, Charles. *Les bourgeois conquérants, XIXe siècle*. Paris: A. Colin, 1957.

————. *The Triumph of the Middle Classes*, trans. by Weidenfeld and Nicolson. London: Weidenfeld and Nicolson, 1966.

Morin, Edgar; Lefort, Claude; and Coudray, J-M. *Mai 1968: la brèche*. Paris: Fayard, 1968.

Mornet, Daniel. *Les Origines intellectuelles de la révolution française*. Paris: A. Colin, 1933.

Myrdal, Gunnar. *Beyond the Welfare State*. New Haven: Yale University Press, 1960.

Nagel, Julian (ed.) *Student Power*. London: Merlin, 1969.

Naville, Pierre. *Le nouveau léviathan*. Paris: M. Rivière, 1957.

Nisbet, Robert. *The Sociological Tradition*. New York: Basic Books, 1967.

————. *Tradition and Revolt*. New York: Random House, 1969.

Organisation for Economic Co-operation and Development. *Reviews of National Science Policy, "United States."* Paris: O.E.C.D., 1968.

Park, Robert E., and Burgess, Ernest W. *Introduction to the Science of Society*. Chicago: University of Chicago Press, 1924.

————, Burgess, Ernest W., and MacKenzie, Roderick D. *The City*. Chicago: University of Chicago Press, 1925.

Parsons, Talcott. *Essays in Sociological Theory*. Glencoe: Free Press, 1949.

————. *The Social System*. Glencoe: Free Press, 1951.

Perroux, François. *L'Économie du 20. siècle*. Paris: P.U.F., 1961.

————. *L'Économie des jeunes nations*. Paris: P.U.F., 1962.

————. *Industrie et création collective*. Paris: P.U.F., 1964.

Pirker, Theo. *Die blinde Macht*. (2 vols.) München: Mercator, 1960.

————, et al. *Arbeiter Management Mibbestimmung*. (Gesellschaft für soziale Betriebspraxis) Stuttgart: Ring Verlag, 1955.

Plessner, Helmuth. *Die verspätete Nation*. Stuttgart: W. Kohlhammer, 1959. (Originally published in 1935 as *Das Schicksal deutschen Geistes im Ausgang seiner bürgerlichen Epoche.*)

Poignant, Raymond. *L'Enseignment supérieur dans les pays du marché commun*. Paris: Institut National de Pédagogie, 1965.

Popitz, Heinrich. *Der entfremdete Mensch*. Basel: Verlag für Recht und Gesellschaft, 1953.

————, et al. *Das Gesellschaftsbild des Arbeiters*. Tübingen: Mohr, 1957.

Popper, Karl. *The Open Society and Its Enemies*. (2 vols.) London: G. Routledge, 1945.

Richta, Radovan. (Equipe de l'Institut de Philosophie de l'Academie des Sciences de Tchecoslovaquie). *La civilisation au carrefour*, trans. by Ludmila Klimova and Jean-Louis Glory. Paris: Anthropos, 1969.

Riesman, David. *Individualism Reconsidered.* Glencoe: Free Press, 1954.

——. *Abundance for What?* Garden City, N. Y.: Doubleday, 1964.

——, et al. *The Lonely Crowd.* New Haven: Yale University Press, 1950.

Rosenberg, Arthur. *Die Entstehung der deutschen Republik 1871– 1918.* Berlin: E. Rowohlt, 1928.

——. *The Birth of the German Republic 1871–1918,* trans. by Ian F. D. Morrow. New York: Oxford University Press, 1931.

——. *Demokratie und Sozialismus.* Amsterdam: A. de Lange, 1938.

——. *Democracy and Socialism,* trans. by George Rosen. New York, London: Knopf, 1939.

——. *Enstehung der Weimarer Republik.* Frankfurt: Europäische Verlagsanstalt, 1961.

Rosenberg, Bernard, and White, David M. (eds.) *Mass Culture.* Glencoe: Free Press, 1957.

Rosenberg, Hans. *Bureaucracy, Aristocracy and Autocracy: The Prussian Experience 1660–1815.* Cambridge: Harvard University Press, 1958.

Saint-Simon, Henri Comte de. *Oeuvres complets.* (6 vols.) Paris: Editions Anthropos, 1966.

Sartre, Jean-Paul. *Critique de la raison dialectique.* Paris: Gallimard, 1960.

——. *Search for a Method,* trans. by Hazel E. Barnes. New York: Knopf, 1963.

——. *Situations.* (7 vols.) Paris: Gallimard, 1947–65.

Schaff, Adam. *Marxismus und das menschliche Individuum.* Wien: Europa Verlag, 1965.

——. *Philosophy of Man.* New York: Dell, 1968.

Schlesinger, Arthur M., Jr. *The Age of Roosevelt.* (3 vols.) Boston: Houghton Mifflin, 1957–60.

——. *A Thousand Days.* Boston: Houghton Mifflin, 1965.

Schmoller, Gustav. *Die Soziale Frage.* München: Duncker, 1918.

Schnabel, Franz. *Deutsche Geschichte im 19. Jahrhundert.* (4 vols.) Freiburg: Herder, 1933–37.

Schumpeter, Joseph. *Capitalism, Socialism and Democracy.* New York: Harper, 1942.

Seligman, Ben B. *Most Notorious Victory.* New York: Free Press, 1966.

Shils, Edward. *The Torment of Secrecy.* Glencoe: Free Press, 1956.

Shonfield, Andrew. *Modern Capitalism*. London: Oxford University Press, 1965.

Sombart, Werner. *Der moderne Kapitalismus*. Leipzig: Duncker, 1902.

——. *Warum gibt es in den Vereinigten Staaten keinen Sozialismus?* Tübingen: Mohr, 1906.

——. *Der Bourgeois*. München: Duncker and Humblot, 1913.

Sontag, Susan. *Against Interpretation*. New York: Farrar, Straus and Giroux, 1966.

——. *Styles of Radical Will*. New York: Farrar, Straus and Giroux, 1969.

Sorel, Georges. *Reflections on Violence*, trans. by T. E. Hulme. London: Allen, 1916.

Spencer, Herbert. *Principles of Sociology*. (3 vols.) New York: Appleton, 1883–97.

Stein, Maurice. *The Eclipse of Community*. Princeton: Princeton University Press, 1960.

Strachey, John. *The Coming Struggle for Power*. New York: Covici-Friede, 1933.

——. *Contemporary Capitalism*. New York: Random House, 1956.

——. *The End of Empire*. New York: Random House, 1959.

Sweezy, Paul M. *The Theory of Capitalist Development*. New York: Oxford University Press, 1942.

——. *The Present as History*. New York: Monthly Review Press, 1953.

——, and Baran, Paul. *Monopoly Capital*. New York: Monthly Review Press, 1966.

Taylor, A. J. P. *The Course of German History*. London: H. Hamilton, 1945.

Thompson, Edward P. *The Making of the English Working Class*. London: Gollance, 1963.

Tönnies, Ferdinand. *Gemeinschaft und Gesellschaft*. (6th ed.) Berlin: K. Curtius, 1926.

——. *Community and Society*, trans. and ed. by Charles P. Loomis. East Lansing: Michigan State University Press, 1957.

Touraine, Alain. *Sociologie de l'action*. Paris: Seuil, 1965.

——. *La Conscience ouvrière*. Paris: Seuil, 1966.

——. *Le Mouvement de mai ou le communisme utopique*. Paris: Seuil, 1968.

——. *La Société post-industrielle*. Paris: Denoël, 1969.

Vaneigem, Raoul. *Traité de savoir-vivre à l'usage des jeunes généra-tions.* Paris: Gallimard, 1967.

Veblen, Thorstein. *The Theory of Business Enterprise.* New York: Scribner, 1904.

———. *Imperial Germany and the Industrial Revolution.* New York: Macmillan, 1915.

———. *The Theory of the Leisure Class.* New York: Macmillan, 1917.

———. *Engineers and the Price System.* New York: B. W. Huebsch, 1921.

Vidich, Arthur, and Bensman, Joseph. *Small Town in Mass Society.* (2d ed.) Princeton: Princeton University Press, 1968.

von Stein, Lorenz Jacob. *Geschichte der sozialen Bewegung in Frankreich.* (new ed., 3 vols.) Hildesheim: Georg Olms, 1959.

———. *History of the Social Movement in France, 1789–1850,* trans. and ed. by Kathe Mengelberg. Totowa, N. J.: Bedminster, 1964.

Wallas, Graham. *The Great Society.* New York: Macmillan, 1914.

Weber, Max. *Gesammelte Aufsätze zur Religionssoziologie.* Tü-bingen: Mohr, 1921.

———. *Wirtschaft und Gesellschaft.* Tübingen: Mohr, 1922.

———. *Economy and Society,* trans. by Gunther Roth and others. (3 vols.) Totowa, N. J.: Bedminister, 1968.

———. *Wirtschaftsgeschichte.* München: Duncker, 1923.

———. *From Max Weber,* trans. and ed. by H. H. Gerth and C. Wright Mills. New York: Oxford University Press, 1946.

———. *Gesammelte Aufsätze zur Soziologie und Sozialpolitik.* Tü-bingen: Mohr, 1924.

———. *General Economic History,* trans. by Frank H. Knight. New York: Collier Macmillan, 1961.

Williams, Raymond. *Culture and Society.* London: Chatto and Win-dus, 1958.

———. *The Long Revolution.* London: Chatto and Windus, 1961.

Williams, William A. *The Contours of American History.* Cleveland: World, 1961.

Zapf, W. (ed.) *Beiträge zur Analyse der deutschen Oberschicht.* Tübingen: Universitat Tübingen Studien und Berichte aus dem soziologischen Seminar, 1964 (#3).

INDEX

] 181 [